From the Readers of E. D. Thompson's
Nashville Nostalgia - (first volume 2003)

"I am writing to express my pleasure and delight for one of the most refreshing, enjoyable strolls I've ever taken by reading and reminiscing over your *Nashville Nostalgia*...with so many wonderful memories it brought back to me... Thank you for a warm, wonderful, delightful reading experience I intend to share and recommend to everyone I know. We in Nashville are truly blessed to have you as our Boswell to remind us of our truly rich heritage and why this city is so very special..."

 Bill Byrge, Nashville, TN

"...When I returned home on December 27, 2003, my son had five Christmas gifts for me to unwrap. One of the gifts was your book, *Nashville Nostalgia*, which I wanted so badly... I really enjoyed seeing the picture of the old National Life Building on page 239. I even saw the window facing Seventh Avenue that I sat in front of for 5 years working as a secretary."

 Edith Trotter, Nashville, TN

"Bob and I just finished reading your book, and we enjoyed it very much. I bought two copies to send to my brothers for their April birthdays."

 Eloise and Bob Taylor, Bellevue, TN

[Excerpts from a letter written to Jeff Thompson by an avid listener to his good music programs on radio WAMB]
"I was surprised to see the Fighter Pilot (WWII) grab the book first. He was flipping through with 'I remember that.' 'Honey, we went there, remember?' Be sure and let your Dad know how much we are enjoying it… Your Dad has no idea what a commotion his book has caused. My cousin received her copy today and is overwhelmed. She wants two more copies for her son and daughter."
Katharen Tate, Smyrna, TN

"My sister, Mary Littell Rust Ellis, brought an autographed copy [*Nashville Nostalgia*] with her to Baltimore when our family gathered for the fifth wedding this year… I began to read it right away in those intervals back at the motel and, if I felt like crying, it was in E. D.'s descriptions of some of the old time Nashville institutions like Candyland and Percy Warner Park. I have so many memories of happy times in Nashville and always speak with pride of my hometown…

"Thank you for writing these things down in such an interesting form. I appreciate having the book, even at a time when I'm disposing of so many books to our library book sale or Goodwill. This one I will enjoy going back to!"
Emmaline Rust Henry, Greencastle, Indiana

More Nashville Nostalgia

By E. D. Thompson

Westview Publishing Co., Inc.
Nashville, Tennessee

First Edition
Printed in the United States of America on alkaline paper

Library of CongressControl Number 2004116437

ISBN 0-9755646-7-6

Acquisitions Editor - Hugh Daniel
Cover design by Melissa Evans and Paula Underwood Winters

Image processing, layout and other pre-press work by Westview Publishing Co., Inc.

Published by
Westview Publishing Co., Inc.
8120 Sawyer Brown Rd., Ste. 107
Nashville, Tennessee 37221
www.westviewpublishing.com

I dedicate this happy journey through
More Nashville Nostalgia

to

Our five wonderful grandchildren
who will be in the next generation of citizens,
to nurture traditions and form nostalgic memories
of their own Nashville.

Kathryn Anne Parsley
Geoffrey Kevin Parsley
Kameron Artyom Parsley
Kelly Ellis Parsley
Kimberly Elva Parsley

E. D. Thompson is uniquely qualified to have written *Nashville Nostalgia* and now this second volume titled *More Nashville Nostalgia*. He was born in Nashville in 1924, and lived here for most of his life. From his memories of an older Nashville have come many interesting stories about old restaurants, hotels, streetcars, schools, music, sports, theatres, businesses, buildings, railroading, old radio, old television, distinguished people, and our old downtown shopping districts.

His weekly columns in the *Westview* Newspaper have stimulated a great deal of interest in how Nashville used to be. E. D. has received many letters and telephone calls from readers telling about how his column has evoked many pleasant memories for them.

E. D. and I were married in New York City on the old NBC television program called *Bride and Groom*. We happily celebrated our 50th wedding anniversary this past August 20, 2004. We have shared together many of these memories and stories which you will read in E. D.'s two volumes of books titled *Nashville Nostalgia* and now this *More Nashville Nostalgia*.

Sonia Anne Young Thompson

Foreword

Welcome to E. D. Thompson's second collection of facts and memories about the Nashville that we remember. If you read *Nashville Nostalgia*, then you know that you are about to add to the knowledge and happiness that you derived from that book. If this volume is your first look back at the Nashville of your childhood and your parents' childhood, then you are about to embark on a journey through the history of a city like no other. *More Nashville Nostalgia* will remind you why Nashville is called the Athens of the South and Music City USA, where your favorite department stores and movie theatres were located, when Hillsboro High School burned down, what big bands played in Nashville, and who Alfred Leland Crabb, Louis Nicholas, Jere Baxter, Ken Bramming, and Bettie Page were.

On every page is a name, a food, a street, or a pastime which will spark a happy memory—and for the parts which are new to you, this book will make you wish you had known them! My father's love for the past is infectious, and you will find yourself sharing his wistful reverence for those sights and sounds which will never come again but which will never leave our memories and our hearts. The only treasure more valuable than Nashville nostalgia is more Nashville nostalgia!

Jeff Thompson
English instructor, Tennessee State University
Weekend announcer,
WAMB-AM 1160 & FM 98.7

A Tribute to the Westview Newspaper

I have had the pleasure of writing a weekly column called "Nashville Nostalgia" for the *Westview* Newspaper in Bellevue, Tennessee (a suburb of Nashville) since May 13, 1999.

Doug Underwood, the founder of the newspaper, started his career in journalism in 1949 with the *Nashville Banner*. From there he went to the *Daily Herald* in Columbia, Tennessee as a photographer, sports writer, and feature writer.

When television came to Nashville, Doug became a highly-regarded news reporter for both WSM-TV, channel 4, and WLAC-TV, channel 5.

Doug's dream was realized in 1978 when he started his own weekly, award winning newspaper in Bellevue, the *Westview*.

I did not know Doug Underwood personally, but I am well aware of the legacy he has left in the foundation of this newspaper.

It has been a pleasure to be associated with Doug's wife, Evelyn Underwood-Miles, who is the newspaper's publisher, and their daughter, Paula Underwood Winters, who is the editor.

Doug Underwood's family is carrying his dream on to mightier heights. The *Westview* Newspaper is excellent in quality, and is serving as a valuable tool in news reporting, enlightenment, and entertainment to the greater Bellevue area and beyond.

E. D. T.

CONTENTS

Introduction

After retiring from the field of education, the business world, and many years as a professional musician, E. D. "Buddy" Thompson began to write a weekly column called "Nashville Nostalgia" for the *Westview* Newspaper in Bellevue, a suburb of Nashville.

The column created a great amount of interest and excitement with the readers, as people seemed to enjoy "looking back" on the old days of Nashville and surrounding area, as well as the nostalgic spirit of the whole country.

From the many letters and telephone calls in response to this column, Thompson also receives many invitations to speak on "Nashville Nostalgia" at clubs and churches.

In the winter of 2001, Thompson was invited to teach a six-weeks class on "Nashville Nostalgia" at Vanderbilt University in their program called "Retirement Learning at Vanderbilt."

Thompson's "Nashville Nostalgia" is heard on a five-minute segment once a week on Vanderbilt's radio station, WRVU-FM 91.1, produced by Ken Berryhill.

Thompson has compiled many stories and information from his weekly columns into this book format revealing nostalgic memories of the old Nashville. His nostalgic reflections carry us even beyond the boundaries of Nashville.

Instead of just stating historical facts, Thompson has involved himself in many of the nostalgic experiences. He has written about many things in which he played a personal role.

He has been able to write about many of his personal experiences and his beloved city because he was born in Nashville in 1924, he attended Nashville public schools and George Peabody College for Teachers in Nashville.

He was a Boy Scout and attended old Camp Boxwell on the Harpeth River, he served in the U. S. Army during World War II, he played professionally as a musician at radio stations WLAC and WSM when live music was used during the Golden Age of Radio, and he was a first clarinetist in the Nashville Symphony Orchestra.

Thompson played in many local dance orchestras. He played for shows coming to Nashville including Holiday on Ice, Ringling Brothers and Barnum & Bailey Circus, and performances featuring such stars as Margaret Whiting, Jimmy Wakely, Kate Smith, Engelbert Humperdinck, Sonny and Cher, Duke Ellington, Ray Stevens, Lorrie Morgan, Bobby Goldsboro, Doc Severinsen, Johnny Cash, and others.

Thompson played on radio, in television, and on recordings. He was around for much of the beginnings of Nashville's Music Row.

Thompson taught music in public schools and on college faculties. He served 30 years as a church choir director, and has had two books published by CSS Publishing Company of Lima, Ohio. *I've Heard That All My Life!* involves familiar expressions from Scripture which are still in use today. *Fire for the Choir* involves the motivation of church choir directors and choir members.

This vast amount of experience has contributed to this second book of nostalgia which will hold the readers' interest, and create a nostalgic spirit which will truly make a person's life happier by remembering.

To further add to the readers' interest, Thompson has

included a section titled "Times, People, Places and Things." This section gives a variety of nostalgic memories rather than centering on just one topic in looking back at the old Nashville days.

Nostalgia can bring happiness to a person's life. This book expresses the love and happiness of the old days of Nashville and beyond.

4

Little Known Facts About Nashville

Nashville is famous in many different ways. During the 1910 Tennessee State Fair, the citizens witnessed the world's first night-time airplane flight which took off from Cumberland Park. The plane was equipped with automobile headlights. The date was June 22, 1910. Old Cumberland Park is where our Tennessee State Fairgrounds are still located.

Many of you will remember the military maneuvers which were held in Tennessee during World War II. Our terrain, climate, and other factors made our area a good practice field for service people learning their jobs which could be transferred later to war areas.

One of the soldiers who emerged from this schooling experience was General George S. Patton, Jr.

Armed Services personnel was huge in our area during World War II. In the summer of 1942, Nashville's banking facilities handled $3,500,000 in cash for the Armed Services moving it from Nashville to Lebanon, and from Lebanon to Army paymasters out in the field. This was one of the largest movements of cash in Nashville's history.

———•———

I love everything about Nashville, even when it rains and when it snows. If anyone ever has a disparaging remark about our weather, simply say, "If you don't like the weather, just wait fifteen minutes and it will change!"

Records show that the coldest day in recent years was on February 2 during the Blizzard of 1951 when the temperature registered 13 degrees below zero. The very next year on July 28, 1952, we experienced the warmest day in recent years with a temperature of 107 degrees!

———•———

Many fine Nashvillians have distinguished themselves in serving our great city and even the country. Many fine citizens called Sylvan Park in West Nashville their home. Of the many notable citizens from Sylvan Park, you will remember these two distinguished people.

Percy Priest, during his younger years, was on the editorial staff of *The Tennessean*. In 1940 he was elected United States Congressman from Nashville's fifth district. He served in Congress from 1940 until 1956, and sponsored the National Mental Health Act.

Lewis Edward Moore was appointed to the office of Postmaster at Nashville by President Harry S. Truman. Moore remained in that post for 22 years, longer than anyone in Nashville history. Moore retired from the Post Office in 1971 with 39 years of service.

Priest and Moore were the best of friends. Lewis Moore served as best man in Percy Priest's wedding.

———•———

Traveller's Rest is the oldest house in the city which is still open to the public. Traveller's Rest was the home of John Overton, a successful lawyer, Tennessee Supreme Court judge, and the main influence for the political advancement of his friend, Andrew Jackson. Traveller's Rest is located near John Overton High School off of Franklin Road.

———•———

John Overton had the grand vision of building a fine hotel before the outbreak of the Civil War. But, it was John Overton's son, John Overton, Jr., who went simply by the name of "The Colonel," who took over his father's financial wealth and businesses, and finished building the magnificent Maxwell House Hotel after the interruption of the Civil War. The hotel was named for the wife of The Colonel who was Harriet Maxwell Overton.

———•———

Printer's Alley downtown got its name from the early printing industry in Nashville. The present Alley is the area where horse drawn wagons rolled in carrying the many printing supplies. In the early days, the area of Printer's Alley encompassed two large newspapers, ten print shops, and thirteen publishers. Even today, Nashville is recognized as one of the leading publishing and printing industry cities in the country.

———•———

Nashvillian Meyer Cohen was a watchmaker and jeweler. After his death, Cohen's widow in 1925 deeded to George Peabody College for Teachers some valuable downtown Nashville real estate having a value of several hundred thousand dollars. With part of the proceeds of the sale of this real estate, Peabody College erected its art building and named it the Cohen Memorial Building which still stands on campus today.

———•———

The palatial mansion called Cheekwood was built in the southwestern suburbs of Nashville by Mr. and Mrs. Leslie Cheek during The Great Depression. Leslie Cheek, of Maxwell House Coffee fame, married Mabel Wood. So, the name Cheek was taken from Leslie, and Wood was his wife's maiden name. Thus, Cheekwood.

Forty years later, the Cheeks' daughter, Mrs. Walter Sharp, gave the estate to the people of Nashville. Now, it is the Tennessee Botanical Garden and Fine Arts Center.

———•———

Some people may not know that William Strickland, who designed our Tennessee State Capitol building, is interred in the walls of the Capitol. He loved the building so much that his request was granted to be buried within the walls of the edifice.

———•———

Downtown in what was once known as Overton Alley, local businessman Daniel C. Buntin created the city's first enclosed shopping mall. We know it as the Arcade between Fourth and Fifth Avenues. It was built in 1903 as a two-tiered shopping mall, and was built as an identical copy of the Galleria Vittorio Emmanuele II arcade in Milan, Italy.

The Arcade caused so much excitement that more than 40,000 people attended the grand opening. At the time, the population of our entire county was about 125,000.

———•———

The Bell South Building, which we fondly call the "Batman Building," is the tallest building in the state. Have you ever just walked around town looking at the building from a variety of locations? The building takes on a totally different look from various angels from which you can see it.

Also, the building's nine-level underground parking garage was the largest building construction excavation ever in the state.

———•———

Everyone should visit the Upper Room Chapel and Museum at 1908 Grand Avenue near the Scarritt-Bennett Center's campus (old Scarritt College.) You don't want to miss seeing the 8-feet-by-17-feet wood carving of Leonardo Da Vinci's painting *The Last Supper.* It is breath-taking.

———•———

Nashville is declared a city of churches. Our city is distinguished by many houses of worship to honor God and nurture the souls of humankind. Vine Street Christian Church moved from old Vine Street (Seventh Avenue) downtown to the present church building on Harding Road. The church was built by architect Edwin Keeble whom I knew. He built the present Hillsboro High School after the original school building burned in 1952. I had the opportunity to help plan the new band room for the new school working with members in Edwin Keeble's company.

Keeble included many unique features in the Vine Street Christian Church on Harding Road. When sitting in the church sanctuary looking at the large clear window with the Christian cross behind the altar, a tree can be seen through that window so one can worship God with an eye on the nature which God created. It is said that people are at their best when they have contact with God's nature.

———•———

Edwin Keeble designed the L & C Tower at the corner of Fourth Avenue, North and Church Street which was constructed in 1956-57. Keeble, with the aid of a Vanderbilt University astronomer, designed the building so as to control the amount of sunlight entering the building.

The placement of windows and vertical aluminum fins resulted in substantial energy savings decades before energy conservation became a national concern.

The high tower was designed to display colors in revealing weather conditions.

———•———

When the Congregation Micah was built on Old Hickory Boulevard, the children in the congregation were asked to write down prayers on paper. Those prayer sheets were then spread out on the ground, and the concrete was poured in on top of them. So, the Rabbi of the congregation can honestly say, "Prayers are the foundation of this building."

———•———

The Downtown Presbyterian Church at the corner of Fifth Avenue, North and Church Street is one of the largest and best preserved examples of Egyptian Revival architecture in the United States.

The building itself was completed in 1851. During the Civil War, the church was used as a hospital by the Union forces. The building underwent extensive remodeling after 1865.

Adelicia Acklen, a grand lady of society in Nashville, donated a 4,000 pound bell to the church which served as the city's fire alarm from 1874 until 1897.

———•———

Our Union Station was built in 1900. Its tower which looms 220 feet above Broad Street was topped by a 19-foot copper statue of Mercury which was the Roman mythological symbol for the messenger.

It took a dare-devil to climb up to the top of the statue and place a light bulb there. As a child, I was told that my uncle, Jim Colvin, who married one of my mother's sisters, agreed to go up there and place the light bulb atop Mercury's statue.

I never knew my Uncle Jim Colvin. I guess he continued to be a dare-devil, because I was told that he died when he fell from a building on which he was working in Birmingham, Alabama.

I am sure that I look at our old Union Station somewhat differently than what others do.

———•———

Vanderbilt University started out with the thoughts of being a Methodist University. Five years after the close of the Civil War, the Methodists made a determined try to establish an institution of higher learning called The Central University of the Methodist Episcopal Church, South. A charter was secured, but money was scarce. Strangely enough, defeat evolved in a rather victorious way.

Bishop Holland Nimmons McTyeire, one of Methodism's commanding figures in Nashville, was working toward the establishment of Central University. It so happened that the Bishop's wife and Mrs. Cornelius Vanderbilt were cousins.

In 1873, there came to the McTyeires an invitation to visit the Vanderbilts in New York. During the visit, the Bishop was very dramatic in describing what seemed to be defeat in establishing Central University in Nashville.

You know the rest of the story. Commodore Cornelius Vanderbilt gave one million dollars to the establishment of the university. Later, the name was changed to Vanderbilt University, and in 1875, classes began to meet on the campus located between 21st Avenue, South and West End Avenue.

By the way, Bishop McTyeire is buried on the Vanderbilt campus, and many pass his grave daily maybe not knowing who he was.

Golden Age
of the Big Bands

Even today, I get a sudden stab of nostalgia
with the sounds in the sands of time.

Francis Craig and His Orchestra with Bob Lamm

Big Band Remotes

As a kid growing up in the thirties and forties, I was struck by a disease brought on by the Big Band remotes on radio from which I have never recovered. I love the Big Bands!

By remotes, I mean that the networks would send out an announcer and an engineer with the remote radio equipment to a hotel or ballroom, and broadcast the band live from that remote location away from the radio studios.

I still can hear fine Big Bands on my old radio tapes. I can sit and listen to Glenn Miller and His Orchestra coming from the Café Rouge of the Pennsylvania Hotel in New York, or Bobby Sherwood and His Orchestra coming from Camp Atterbury, Indiana on January 2, 1945 on the program called *Victory Parade of Spotlight Bands* during World War II. I can enjoy them today just like I was listening to them back when they were live

Also, Nashville is fortunate in having a nostalgic Big Band radio station. We can listen to old radio and the Big Bands on WAMB-AM 1160 and FM 98.7.

The Big Bands (c. 1930s and 1940s) had a national outlet for their promotion. When a bandstand was built in a hotel or ballroom, it was wired for radio broadcasting.

I remember hearing Benny Goodman from the Hotel New Yorker, Tommy Dorsey from the Glen Island Casino, Harry James from the Hollywood Palladium, Chuck Foster from the roof of the Hotel Peabody in Memphis, Cab Calloway from the Savoy Ballroom, Gene Krupa from the Hotel Astor Roof in New York City, and many others.

There was something electrifying about hearing that opening theme song of the band. The Big Bands played such great arrangements (which we now call charts) with such clean ensemble, intonation, balance and phrasing. Yes, as a kid, I was struck. All I could think about was becoming a musician.

During those Big Band days, a radio network such as NBC Red or Blue, CBS, or the Mutual Broadcasting System would send their people out on a remote. Great excitement would be in the air as everybody would be crowded around the bandstand, or around the radio for those listening.

When the time came for the broadcast, you might hear the announcer with his pear-shaped tones say something like, "Coming to you from Frank Dailey's Meadowbrook on Route 23, just off the Pompton Turnpike in Cedar Grove, New Jersey, we present the music of Charlie Barnet and His Orchestra."

Then, you would hear his theme song. The crowd would cheer. It was live. It was exciting. Yes, electrifying!

The bands got paid for playing before the audience, of course. But, more importantly, the bands got to publicize their latest recordings. They made stars of their vocalists and instrumentalists by way of the radio remotes that were broadcast over the networks to the nation.

Every band wanted to play the ballrooms and hotels that were connected coast-to-coast by radio wires. A band could become famous overnight which would result in increased sales of records and demands for personal appearances.

There is an interesting story about Glenn Miller when his band first played the Meadowbrook. Frank Dailey's Meadowbrook was a very prestigious engagement. Every band wanted to be booked into the Meadowbrook. From the

Meadowbrook, radio wires ran in every direction across the country.

Back at that time, Glenn Miller was not as well known as were Tommy Dorsey, Benny Goodman, Larry Clinton, Kay Kyser, Fats Waller, Cab Calloway, Jimmy Lunceford, and others.

The Glenn Miller band was booked into the Meadowbrook in March of 1939. Larry Clinton and His Orchestra, who were riding high on their big recordings of "Deep Purple" and "My Reverie," had preceded Glenn at the Meadowbrook. When Larry Clinton announced on the microphone that Glenn Miller would be following him into the Meadowbrook, some people in the audience called out, "Who's Glenn Miller?"

The Meadowbrook was a big, barn-like place. It had a large dance floor with the bandstand at one end, and a balcony running around the other three sides. The acoustics were superb. Behind the bandstand were installed those radio wires.

When Glenn and his band came in for their booking, the people at the Meadowbrook instantly loved his music. Frank Dailey picked up the band's option even before the end of the first week, extending the four weeks' engagement to seven weeks.

Glenn Miller did six broadcasts each week. People all over the country soon heard the Glenn Miller sound. The announcer would come on the air with excitement in his voice. Then, Glenn's theme, "Moonlight Serenade," with clarinet lead above four saxophones filled the airwaves. No one would ever again say, "Who's Glenn Miller?"

Sixth Floor of the Warner Building

In December of 1942, during the Golden Age of the Big Bands, I was a freshman music major on a scholarship at George Peabody College for Teachers in Nashville. Woodwind professor C. B. Hunt, Jr. said, "E. D., you say that you need to make more money, right?"

I quickly replied, "Yes Sir, I certainly do. I need to help support my mother." My father had died when I was sixteen years old and a junior at West End High School.

Professor Hunt with a real sense of interest continued, "Why don't you join the musicians' union and become eligible to be hired by local bands?"

Professor Hunt said, "You need to have a union musician sponsor your membership and sign for you. I would be glad to do that for you."

C. B. Hunt played saxophone at WSM radio on a network show called *Sunday Down South* sponsored by the Lion Oil Company. Beasley Smith was the director of that studio orchestra.

Prior to conducting at WSM radio, Beasley Smith had a fine dance orchestra. To reveal the quality of his band, I know that Charlie Barnet played in the sax section of his band for a time, and Beasley's drummer for a time was Ray McKinley.

I was going from one high to another. "Professor Hunt, that is terrific! How much will it cost me to join the union?"

Professor Hunt enthusiastically stated, "I think the initial membership fee is about twenty-eight dollars, which includes a small amount of dues for the first year."

"Golly, I don't know."

"Oh, don't worry. You will make that back after playing two or three jobs. The union will let you pay it monthly, anyway."

I went home and explained everything to my mother. Her reaction was, "Well, I think it will be O. K. Professor Hunt certainly seems to have a lot of confidence in you."

The very next day, my mother and I took the Belmont Heights streetcar to downtown Nashville. Mother went shopping, and I rushed over to the Warner Building at the corner of Sixth Avenue and Church Street. The musicians' union office was located on the sixth floor of the Warner Building.

I entered the union office and was greeted by a distinguished looking gentleman. I said, "My name is E. D. Thompson, and I am…"

The gentleman quickly smiled and said, "I am George Cooper, president of local 257. You are the kid that C. B. Hunt was telling me about."

"Yes sir, that's right."

Mr. Cooper said, "E. D., meet Bob Payne. Bob is the secretary-treasurer of our local, and he can fill you in on everything you need to know about joining."

Mr. Bob Payne was a very soft-spoken person who moved slowly in seeking certain papers to give to me. I learned over the many years to come that Mr. Payne's standard for accuracy was extremely high. This gave him an attitude of easiness, slowness, and accuracy. I took a liking to Bob Payne right away.

Mr. Payne said, "E. D., how old are you?"

I replied, "I'm eighteen."

Mr. Payne looking at me over his glasses said, "Since you

are not twenty-one, you will have to get your parent to sign this sheet giving you permission to join."

I replied, "Oh, that's no problem. My mother is down-town shopping right now. I'll go get her signature."

I almost literally flew out of the office. I took the elevator down to the first floor of the Warner Building and stepped out onto Church Street. Then, I raced through the streets to locate my mother.

I went down to Fifth Avenue and looked around for her. I dashed into Loveman's at the corner of Fifth and Union. Then, I went back up to Church Street. I darted into Cain-Sloan and still couldn't find her. I then went up to Castner-Knott Dry Goods Company at the corner of Seventh and Church. She was not there. Finally, I found my mother as she was coming out of the Watkins Building on Church Street where she had just paid our light bill.

Mother signed the sheet, and I was back at the union office in no time. My excitement wouldn't allow me to wait even a minute.

I gave Bob Payne the paper with my mother's signature. Bob explained other things to me about the union. Then, I handed Mr. Payne five dollars as a first payment on my membership fees. Bob wrote out my first union card "Local 257 of the American Federation of Musicians."

Going back down on the elevator, and arriving on the Nashville streets, I wasn't at all in the big hurry as before. Now, I had sort of a strut to my walk, and was enjoying very high spirits. I was now a union musician!

My First Big Band Job

In December of 1942, World War II was on. I was enrolled as a freshman music major at George Peabody College in Nashville.

Our neighbor, James Kilgore, who lived two doors down from us on Paris Avenue, was called into the Army. Before he left for duty, he brought me two big boxes of his wonderful Big Band 78 RPM records. James said to me, "I won't need these records until after I come home from the war. I thought you might like to have them and play them on your Victrola. Keep them for me."

What a thrill this brought to my life. I would put those old records on our wind-up Victrola and play and play them. Often, I would conduct the bands, utilizing all of the accents and dynamics with my hand movements as I heard the great bands perform. Then, I would pick up one of my horns and play along with the record.

One of the records that James had left with me was the recording of Artie Shaw's "Concerto for Clarinet." I learned to play most of that clarinet solo along with the record.

It wasn't too many days after I had joined the musicians' union when I received a telephone call.

"Hello."

The voice on the other end of the line said, "May I speak to Buddy Thompson, please?" Among my family members and many musicians, I am known as Buddy Thompson.

I quickly replied, "This is he."

"Buddy, my name is Tommy Witherspoon. I am the manager of Horace Holly's Orchestra. Have you accepted a job yet for New Year's Eve?"

"No sir, I haven't."

"We need another sax man on that night. Can you take the job with Horace Holly and His Orchestra at the Old Hickory Country Club?"

"Yes sir, I certainly can."

"Very good. The job will be from ten until two. We need you on alto sax and clarinet. Wear a tuxedo, white shirt, and a black bow tie. Be on the stand and ready to tune-up at nine forty-five."

"Yes sir, Mr. Witherspoon. I'll be there. You can count on me. I'll get there early."

I guess every musician remembers his first Big Band job. I can remember every detail of mine. My first Big Band job as a union musician was on the night of New Year's Eve, December 31, 1942. I remember some of the musicians on the band.

Two other sax men on the band were this Tommy Witherspoon who had called me on the phone, and tenor saxophone player Bob "Hamp" Young. I certainly didn't know at the time in 1942 when I first met Bob Young that in less than twelve years, I would marry his sister. Her name was Sonia Anne Young.

The fine trumpet man on that job was Dean Gatwood. His father had been the head of the music department at Peabody College back before my time.

The drummer on that job was Otto Bash. Otto was and is a fine drummer and singer. Otto played and recorded with Papa John Gordy, Del Wood, and others. Otto had a recording contract with RCA Victor Records as a singer. Otto later became an officer with the Nashville Association of Musicians, Local 257.

I remember the bass man was Goldie Stewart, and the very fine piano man was Billy Mabry. Horace Holly fronted the band and sang. He was a very good showman. People loved his music. I was playing quite a bit while I was a freshman music student at the college.

In April of 1943, I, along with others as members of the Army Enlisted Reserved Corps attending Peabody and Vanderbilt, went into active duty in the Army. We were sent to Fort Oglethorpe, Georgia where we would be processed.

While in the mess hall on K. P. duty one night, who should I bump into but Tommy Witherspoon with whom I had played that New Year's Eve job with the Horace Holly Orchestra.

When Tommy saw me, he said, "You are just the guy we need!" It seems that they needed another saxophone player in the post dance orchestra. Tommy told me that he would tell his commanding officer, and he would send papers over the next day to assign me to the band.

But, this is another story. Before I could get the orders that next day to play in the band, I was shipped out to Camp Grant, near Rockford, Illinois!

But, believe me, that still didn't remove music from my life!

The Nashville We Love

From a small but charming little town
To even a quaint, hospitable southern city today.

Church Street looking east

Do You Remember These Old Nashville Names?

Our nostalgic spirits can grab a glimmer of Nashville nostalgia just by remembering some of the great, old Nashville names which you may not have thought about in years.

During the growth of Nashville, we have had our share of distinguished, eminent, famous, reputable, noble, and lofty citizens, including the celebrated.

Ben West was elected mayor of Nashville in the early 1950s. He was famous for his blue-dotted bow ties.

Clifford Allen used to be Davidson County's tax assessor. Beverly Briley served as Davidson County judge for many years. Then, in 1963, he became the first mayor of the newly formed Metropolitan Government of Nashville.

George H. Cate, Jr. was the first vice-mayor of Metro Government. Jerry Atkinson then served as vice-mayor followed by David Scobey.

Tony Sudekum was a young businessman who opened Nashville's first movie theatre in 1907, a nickelodeon called the Dixie, located on Fifth Avenue, North. He went on to establish a chain of theatres in several states.

Ed Temple, as Tennessee State University women's track coach, placed 33 ladies on Olympic teams, and they won 11 gold medals. One of his athletes was Wilma Rudolph.

Robert Penn Warren was a writer associated with Vanderbilt University who made important contributions to American literature. Warren won the Pulitzer Prize for fiction in 1947 with his novel, *All the King's Men.*

J. Percy Priest was a United States Congressman who died in 1956 while in office. One of our lakes and a dam which we use today are named for him.

J. Carlton Loser served as our Attorney General, served 22 years as county prosecutor, and later became a United States Congressman.

Luke Lea owned *The Nashville Tennessean* newspaper. Two strong journalists he hired were Edward Carmack and sports editor Grantland Rice. Silliman Evans bought *The Nashville Tennessean* in 1937.

James G. Stahlman succeeded his grandfather as publisher of the *Nashville Banner.*

Claude Jarman, Jr. was a ten-year-old student at Eakin Elementary School who won a special Academy Award after he starred with Gregory Peck in the 1945 movie titled *The Yearling.*

Johnny Beazley was an alumnus of Hume-Fogg High School, and became a pitcher in major league baseball. When Johnny pitched for the St. Louis Cardinals, he beat the New York Yankees twice in the 1942 World Series.

The Cheek family, within the Cheek-Neal Company, gave Maxwell House Coffee to the world. Leslie Cheek and his wife built a mansion in the southwestern suburbs of Nashville back during The Great Depression. Years later, Cheek's daughter, Mrs. Walter Sharp, gave the estate to the people of Nashville. We know it as Cheekwood where we can enjoy the beautiful botanical gardens and fine arts. Walter Sharp was the primary leader in establishing our present Nashville Symphony Orchestra.

Do you remember Elmer Hinton who wrote a column in *The Tennessean* for many years called "Down to Earth?"

Ira North was the minister at the Madison Church of

Christ for many years. He started the "Amazing Grace Bible Class."

Dr. Matthew Walker was the chairman of the Department of Surgery at Meharry Medical College. Walker Clinic was named in honor of him.

Athens Clay Pullias was a David Lipscomb College educator, and also wrote a column for *The Tennessean.*

Nashville has had a number of weather reporters on television. Do you remember when channel 4 had Bill Williams? He appeared also on WSM radio's morning "Waking Crew," and was known as the "rhyming weatherman."

In 1943, Cornelia Fort was the first woman pilot to die in the service of her country. We named an airport over in East Nashville in honor of her.

Dr. Dorothy Brown was the first African-American woman to practice general surgery in the South. She was also the first African-American woman ever elected to the Tennessee State General Assembly. My wife, Sonia, sang in a choral group with her.

Do you remember Super Shan, a broadcaster on the old WMAK radio station? His real name was Scott Shannon.

Jim Kent, a Bellevue resident, was at WSIX radio for many years.

Did you ever read the advice column by Jean Bruce which appeared for many years in *The Sunday Tennessean?* Do you remember the well-known local actress and WSM-TV *Noon Show* personality by the name of Barbara Moore? She died in the 1970s. Her husband, Rick Moore, was in television, also.

Of course, you remember Wayne Oldham, the restaurateur and musician, who was always seen wearing a homburg.

James Carroll Napier, a lawyer, served for eight years on the City Council. He was prominent in the creation of Pearl

High School and Meigs High School for African-Americans back during the days of segregation.

Nashvillian Lou Graham won the PGA U. S. Open golf tournament back in 1975. Do you remember Paul Eels? Paul is a former Vanderbilt sportscaster who moved from WSM-TV to the state of Arkansas to call the ball games for the Razorbacks of Arkansas. Paul was noted for using the phrase, "Holy Smokes!"

Do you remember who succeeded Bob Polk as head basketball coach at Vanderbilt? It was Roy Skinner.

In the old days, Marjorie Cooney was a staff member at WSM radio, and was probably the nation's first regular female news anchor. You may remember the radio program, *A Woman Looks at the News*. Marge was a close friend of Fanny Rose Shore (Dinah Shore) when both of them were at WSM radio. Marge was a fine pianist, and did some piano work at the radio station.

When our present Nashville Symphony Orchestra began in 1946, Marge also worked as the orchestra manager. She handed me my pay check each month when I played in the symphony.

Also, Marge Cooney worked at WSM television. She was the director of a children's show on channel 4 in the afternoons with Tom Tichenor and his puppets. I wrote and performed on one of those shows. Marge was a tough boss.

In 1959, when I was working in Chattanooga, my wife and I went to the Read House Hotel to attend a reception for volunteer workers in the Community Concert Series organization. When we got there, who should walk in but Marjorie Cooney! She had taken a job with that organization which sponsored concerts all over the country. What a great surprise for us to see a familiar Nashville face.

Hank Hillin was a former sheriff and former FBI agent who wrote the book titled *FBI Codename TENNPAR*. Garner Robinson served as one of our sheriffs. Another sheriff was Leslie Jett.

John Trotwood Moore was a Nashville author, editor, and State Librarian whose home was located on Granny White Pike near Lone Oak Road. At that location today we have the John Trotwood Moore School. By the way, that location was not far from where Pat Boone's mother and father continued to live after Pat moved to Hollywood.

Of course, you remember when Richard Fulton was our United States Congressman for the fifth district, and then became the mayor of Nashville. My wife, Sonia, was a school mate of Dick Fulton at East Nashville High School.

Here is something about Dick that you may not remember. When Dick Fulton played football at East Nashville High School, he was an All-Southern guard, and once he blocked three punts in one game.

———————•———————

I enjoy learning about the personalities and families from the old days of Nashville. Many of our structures and places remain named for the old families which make the stories about them seem like the events happened just a short time ago.

Westview Newspaper's illustrious sports editor, Dick Green, and I have had many conversations on topics from Air Force bases, to Strategic Air Command, to the War on Terrorism, to football. In fact, we have solved many of the world's problems!

One day Dick reminded me of a man named Walker from Old Nashville which he had studied at Vanderbilt in a history class. William Walker was born in Nashville. He was a military adventurer, and became an international sensation as a soldier of fortune. Walker tried to conquer parts of Mexico. In fact, he did make himself ruler of Nicaragua after leading a successful revolution there. He served as the president of Nicaragua from 1856 until 1857. Then, he was forced to leave by the people of Nicaragua.

Walker tried to regain power in Nicaragua in1860, but was captured and executed by a firing squad in Honduras.

William Walker was a good friend of Joseph and Adelicia Acklen prior to the Civil War, and was their guest many times at the Belmont Mansion which sits atop 16th Avenue, South and Wedgewood Avenue. Walker is a prominent character in Alfred Leland Crabb's historical novel, *Dinner at Belmont.*

Francis Fogg was the first chairman of the city school board in Nashville. Back during the formative years of our city, Francis Brinley Fogg practiced law from an office on Cherry Street (Fourth Avenue, North) near Deaderick Street. His son, Henry Middleton Rutledge Fogg, was his law partner.

Francis Fogg's wife and mother of Henry was Mary Middleton Rutledge Fogg. The story is told that Henry Fogg was killed in Kentucky during the Civil War while serving as an aide to Confederate General Felix Zollicoffer.

Within a few minutes of Henry's death, the general had Henry's body delivered back to Nashville to the Fogg home on Church Street. The Fogg home was roughly where the old Watkins Institute building was located, and where our new Nashville Public Library presently stands.

The next time you go downtown to the new library, think of how close you will be to the Old Nashville and the Fogg's home.

No, Nashville is not so old that we can't walk among places and things and see some of the same sights that citizens of the Old Nashville saw.

I have mentioned just a handfull of names from our Nashville. There are thousands more who made definite contributions to our city.

Did I See You at the Happiness Club?

How I loved to go to the movies when I was growing up. And, I go way back to the ten cent movie days which included the "Popeye Club" at the old Paramount Theatre. Later, admission at theatres was twenty-five cents if we went in before five o'clock in the afternoon. After five and for the night showings, the cost went to a staggering forty cents!

I loved going to the movies downtown. I loved the old Paramount, the Loew's, the Knickerbocker, and the old Princess Theatres. Being a young, student musician, I loved to watch and listen to the musicians in the pit orchestra at the Princess Theatre play the overture. It was a thrill to see the lights come up, the curtain rise, and then the great music and acts on stage.

I miss going to the neighborhood theatres, too. We had the Melrose, Belmont, Green Hills, Belle Meade, Madison, Woodland, Inglewood, Ritz, Roxy, Elite, on and on. Today, when we go to a movie, we get to see only the feature film. Back in my time, we got to see a cartoon, news reel, travelogue, a Robert Benchley or Pete Smith short subject special, and maybe a cliff-hanging serial, plus the feature film.

Maybe I miss the excitement of many Hollywood musical productions on the screen which included no un-redeeming violence, no inferior sexual instruction for our youth, and no language which would embarrass every family member while on a family outing.

When the Bookstar Bookstore was located in the old Belle Meade Theatre, I enjoyed strolling in and remembering the old theatre. Where the great silver screen used to stand in the theatre showing life-size figures of Loretta Young, Myrna Loy, Andy Devine, Rita Hayworth, Tyrone Power, Clark Gable, Cary Grant, and a legion of others, had become the periodical section of the bookstore.

Belle Meade Theatre after becoming a bookstore

Thankfully, we still had some creative visionaries in Nashville during the occupancy of the Bookstar Bookstore who chose to keep some of the Belle Meade Theatre's outside structure, a portion of the lobby, and the great "Wall of Fame" possessing dozens of photos that Nashville's beloved Mr. E. J. Jordan took of the many stars who visited the Belle Meade Theatre over the years.

The Belle Meade Theatre's opening took place on May 1, 1940. Mr. E. J. Jordan was the theatre manager from 1940 until 1967. Many of us or our children attended his "Happiness Club" which met at the theatre every Saturday afternoon. Mr. Jordan was determined to keep good order in the theatre when it was filled with enthusiastic and energetic kids. You may remember Mrs. Drake who served as a matron to help keep good order. The Belle Meade policeman in charge of security was affectionately known as "Big Joe."

The Belle Meade Theatre probably holds some kind of record for a long run of a movie. *The Sound of Music* ran for about six straight months at the theatre.

The Bookstar Bookstore kept Mr. Jordan's Wall of Fame in the lobby with all of the photographs of the movie stars. At the opening of the theatre in 1940, Irene Dunne affixed the first signature and photo for the Wall of Fame. Since then, 175 other stars signed their photos in person for the "Wall of Fame."

Today, at the writing of this book about nostalgia, the old movie palace of many memories sits

*Belle Meade Theatre Manager
E.J. Jordan's Wall of Fame*

vacant on Harding Road looking rather lonesome. Even the old Moon Drugstore which used to sit next door departed that area some time ago. Moon's was not just a drugstore, either. It was a meeting place. It was a great place to get sandwiches and delights from the soda fountain while you socialized with friends.

It has been reported that a new office building will be constructed at the location of the old Belle Meade Theatre. I have no idea if sentimental parts of the old theatre or Mr. E. J. Jordan's Wall of Fame will be kept or not. One thing that can't be torn down is our nostalgic memory.

Nashville's Publishing Industry Continues

Almost from the beginning, Nashville has been a center for publishing and printing. Printer's Alley downtown gets its name because that area of the old Nashville was the center of printing and publishing. Horse-drawn wagons brought in all of the printing supplies to the Printers Alley area.

At one time, the *Nashville Banner* and *The Tennessean* newspapers had their offices in that area of the city.

The *Nashville Banner* was founded in 1876. *The Tennessean* was first published in 1907.

Edward Bushrod Stahlman, who was a former L & N Railroad official, published the *Nashville Banner*. E. B. Stahlman published the newspaper for 37 years. After that, his grandson, James Geddes Stahlman, published the newspaper for another 42 years. Most of us knew him as Jimmy Stahlman.

We still have a twelve-story building downtown named for E. B. Stahlman. The Stahlman Building on Union Street was one of Nashville's first skyscrapers.

During the old days of Nashville, more than a dozen firms published a rich variety of printed materials. This included some popular magazines such as *Southern Agriculturalist*, *Trotwood's Monthly*, *Southern Lumberman*, *Confederate Veteran*, and a publication called *Bob Taylor's Magazine*.

Some of the large quantities of printing materials were done by religious publishing houses. Nashville as a religious publishing center included firms such as Publishing House for the Methodist Episcopal Church South, the Sunday School board of the Southern Baptist Church, the National Baptist Publishing Board, the Cumberland Presbyterian Publishing House, the Gospel Advocate, the National Baptist Union, and the Penecostal Mission Publishing Company. The publishing of music was and is a large portion of religious publishing houses.

I have read that the Anglo-American folk music came to the Nashville Bluffs with the settlers, and music publishing is said to have begun in 1824 with a book of hymns titled *The Western Harmony.*

One of the pioneers in religious music publishing in Nashville was the John T. Benson Publishing Company. His son and grandsons have kept the tradition alive.

One of the early pop and country music publishers began in 1942 as the Acuff-Rose Publishing Company. Fred Rose was a songwriter who had an afternoon show on WSM radio. He sang a lot of his songs accompanied by piano. He wrote "Deed I Do," "Blue Eyes Cryin' in the Rain," "Tears on My Pillow," a song we associate with Sophie Tucker titled "Red Hot Mama," a song he wrote for Gene Autry titled, "Be Honest with Me" which was nominated for an Academy Award in 1940, "It's a Sin" which was a 1947 number one song for Eddy Arnold, and many other songs.

I remember hearing Fred Rose sing and play the piano on WSM when I was a kid. I enjoyed his program, because I was trying to write songs, too.

Fred Rose teamed with Roy Acuff to develop a very successful music publishing business. After Fred's death, his son, Wesley Rose, continued the operation of the company.

Richard Henry Boyd founded the National Baptist Publishing Board, which was the first African-American institution of its kind. Dr. R. H. Boyd became the first editor-in-chief, and issued the first publications in 1897.

Today, Dr. T. B. Boyd III carries on the family tradition of publishing for the National Baptist denomination.

I had the pleasure of working with Dr. T. Boyd and Mr. John T. when hymn writer Elmo Mercer and I helped edit the

National Baptist Publishing Board

New National Baptist Hymnal back in 1977.

Some 24 years later, I was asked to be the final editor for the 800-page *New National Baptist Hymnal, 21st Century Edition.* It was a pleasure to work once again with Dr. T. B. Boyd III and Mr. John T. Benson III. This new 21st century hymnal was published in October of 2001.

The publishing and printing tradition continues in Nashville today with newspapers, magazines, books, brochures, large religious publishing houses, and music publishing. Thanks to Doug Underwood, his family, and the *Westview* Newspaper, for which I am a columnist, as being a part of this Nashville tradition.

Today, the varied amount of publishing and printing locally places Nashville among the nation's leaders in the publishing and printing industry.

NEW TOWN and
The Richland Park Neighborhood

After the Civil War, the South needed to recover finan-
cially. After a number of years, people felt that new industry is
what was needed to produce financial help. Citizens felt that a
new southern, industrial city could create jobs and money for
development and expansion.

A group of business leaders led by industrialist Henry M.
Pierce organized the Nashville Land Improvement Company in
1887. Some early investors were railroad executive E. W. Cole,
former state treasurer William Morrow, and Willard Warner
who was the general manager of the Nashville Iron, Steel and
Charcoal Company.

The site of the new manufacturing city of the South was
chosen. It was decided to develop an industrial town about
three miles from the Tennessee State Capitol building in
Nashville. The new town was to be West Nashville. However,
the citizens began to call it simply NEW TOWN.

According to the writings of the late Sarah Foster Kelley
in her book titled *West Nashville, Its People and Environs*, NEW
TOWN was to become a center of the charcoal iron business
where advantage could be taken of its mineral resources of
iron, coal, and hardwood. Also, the town would be located near
the cultural center of Nashville. Development soon began on
a stock farm called Richland.

A surveyor was hired to plan a grid of streets. Streets

running north and south were numbered. Streets running east and west were named for the states of the Union.

As time passed, NEW TOWN (West Nashville) developed into a number of neighborhoods. Richland Park Neighborhood was one of them, and is the oldest existing site in West Nashville.

On the south side of the Park, a row of Victorian brick homes were built along Park Avenue. On the north side would be the business district. Over the years, Richland Park has experienced such scenes as ice cream festivals, foot races, church socials, family reunions, band concerts, story hours, as well as free silent and talking movies.

A swimming pool was located at the eastern side of the park. Over the years, citizens have enjoyed a playground, tennis matches, croquet games, baseball games, as well as ping-pong and billiard games in the community center. A small house, located in the center of the playground, held baseball bats, softballs, gloves, croquet mallets, and various other balls and sporting equipment..

Some of you may know Jim Booth who is a good West Nashville citizen and a member of the Greatest Generation. Jim was in the Navy during World War II and was assigned to the USS New Orleans, a heavy cruiser in the Pacific. Jim told me that his father, George Booth, was one of the motormen who drove the old Sylvan Park Dinky back in the old days. It was a small streetcar which transported passengers between Charlotte Pike and present Nebraska Avenue.

Jim also told me that he practically grew up in the grocery store at 42nd Avenue and Charlotte which was owned by his grandfather. That old building still stands at 42nd and Charlotte.

In 1927, the Crescent Amusement Company opened the Elite Theatre on Charlotte Pike across from the Park with Tony Sudekum as owner and manager. There were two shows a day. A Seeburg organ played during the intermission. The aisles were covered with linoleum. A power projector was used on the full-size screen. There was no air-conditioning. Fans were used to circulate the air.

From Richland Park showing the Elite Theatre

Third National Bank got its start in West Nashville at the Elite Theatre in 1948. Andrew B. Gibson, known to the citizens as Andy, was put in charge of the pilot project. In 1958, a new building of Third National Bank was constructed up Charlotte Pike. Mrs. Margaret Allen served some 32 years as the banker's secretary. Being a West Nashville resident, she attended old Bellevue High School.

In 1928, a junior high school was opened offering grades

seven, eight, and nine. The structure was named for Mrs. Corinne Lieberman Cohn, a former member of the City Board of Education. Professor Jonas H. Sykes, who had come to NEW TOWN in 1896 as head of the old West Nashville High School (which was later renamed Cockrill School), was made principal of this new Cohn Junior High School. Jonas Sykes and his wife, Allie, sang in the choir at the West Nashville Methodist Church as well as taught Sunday School classes.

In the Fall of 1939, Professor Sykes retired as principal of Cohn Junior High School. He died in 1941, and by unanimous decision of the Board of Education, the new athletic field which was constructed in old Clifton Park serving both Cockrill and Cohn Schools, was named Sykes Field.

The new principal of Cohn would be William Rayburn Rochelle. Tenth, eleventh, and twelfth grades were soon added to form Cohn High School. Professor Rochelle was principal of Cohn when I taught band at Hillsboro High School. Hillsboro played Cohn in football.

After nearly thirty years, in 1965 Professor Rochelle retired. The beloved Professor Rochelle was especially proud of Cohn's graduates. He saw many of his students become doctors, lawyers, ministers, engineers, administrators, aviators, and educators. Two former Cohn High students are presently serving as judges in Metro. They are Judge Bill Higgins and Judge Randall Wyatt.

Richland Park fell into decay by 1960. The old band shell and recreation center were converted into a library. Richland Park Branch Library was opened in October of 1961. The building was renovated and enlarged in 1979. Librarian Lucille Sterling served the library for 17 years. Following her untimely death in 1984, Charles W. Meeker, Jr. served as librarian.

Some of you probably knew West Nashville's Bessie

Redmond. She was an active worker in West Nashville before passing away in 2003. Bessie used to work on the annual "Old Timers Day" celebration, and was very successful in her work for the Richland Park Library.

Some years back, there was talk about closing down three or four community libraries, and Richland Park was one of them. In working to keep the library open, Bessie got petitions signed at grocery stores and every other place she went. Bessie revealed that 25 different schools were using the Richland Park Library. Bessie attended meetings held by Mayor Bredesen, and her daughter told me that even a TV station came out and interviewed her. Bessie was one of the great supporters that kept the library open. Her daughter, Judith Redmond, still lives in West Nashville.

We can say that many citizens have made West Nashville proud of the service they have rendered in our city, state, and even the world.

Little Salt Lick Revisited

During the days when automobiles were rather new, roads were very poor, and passenger trains were popular, many Nashvillians during the hot summers headed out to one of the great resorts surrounding our city. Do you remember summers at Horn Springs, Ruskin Cave, Dunbar Cave, Beersheba, Monteagle, Rock Island, Jefferson Springs, and Red Boiling Springs among others?

My family made trips to Red Boiling Springs in the 1930s. My uncle was a barber at The Palace Grand Hotel there. The Palace was the largest hotel in Red Boiling Springs with 184 rooms.

As a child, I remember the crowds of people, and the large porches extending around the hotels. Some people would spend their whole time just a-sittin' and a-rockin' in those chairs on the porches.

In the old days, we enjoyed some good, southern cooking at the hotels. When we entered a hotel dining room, we sat down to a delicious, delightful, delectable feast for which defining memorable dining words could not adequately express.

Many visitors there enjoyed the bath houses with healthy, healing mineral waters. Other activities were swimming, horseshoe pitching, horseback riding, and hiking.

My wife, Sonia, told me that her mother and relatives used to pack their travel trunks each summer, take the train from Union Station, and spend a whole month in Red Boiling Springs, Tennessee.

One day several years back, I, along with Sonia, my wife, and Elva, my sister, drove up to the renowned Red Boiling Springs which I had not visited in almost seventy years.

Back in the town's glory days of the 1920s and 1930s, there were 13 Grand Hotels in Red Boiling Springs. We were so pleased to see that three of the old hotels were still there. We saw the Donoho Hotel, the Armour's Hotel, and the old Cloyd Hotel.

Driving into Red Boiling Springs, I was struck with several childhood flashbacks. I remembered the Little Salt Lick Creek which ran right through the town with the hotels and homes on each side.

I was reminded that there were four kinds of mineral water which the local people referred to as black water, white water, red water, plus double and twist. I asked one lady why one was called double and twist. She responded, "Well, that is what you do when you drink it!"

We toured the town with all of its quaintness and the surrounding uniqueness of our Tennessee's back woods. We drove over and through a covered bridge. We saw the lush farmland nestled between the majestic rolling hills.

Unfortunately, many of the old mineral pump houses were in disrepair, and so were many of the old and famous bath houses. However, we could see remnants of them, remembering how stately and grand things were back in their glory years and in our youth. However, mineral water is still there.

The old Palace Hotel has been torn down. A nice brick nursing home now sits at that site in town. Appropriately enough, the nursing home is named The Palace.

Before we left town, we wanted to have a meal of great southern cooking which we discovered was still there.

The old Cloyd Hotel, sitting with all of its grandeur atop

a shaded hill, was open for dining. The name of the old hotel had been changed to The Thomas House. However, it still wore the old face of the Cloyd which was first built in 1890. After it burned, it was rebuilt in 1924 with its present 54 rooms.

We were welcomed into the great dining room, and were treated with the service and the kind of delectable food that reigned there as we remembered almost seventy years before.

As my wife, my sister, and I drove away from this beautiful world of memories, I took one last look at the peaceful and flowing stream of water running through this quaint town, and thought of how as a child I used to stick my feet in that old Little Salt Lick Creek. Some things never change.

The Ever-Changing Music Row

When I heard that a "condemned" sign had been placed by a Metro inspector on the glass front doors of a large, black and white building in East Nashville, a lot of nostalgic memories flooded my mind. I remember when that old building in the Five Points commercial district of East Nashville was the Woodland Theatre.

The local area merchants had hopes that the nearly century-old building would stay and be developed in a way to preserve the neighborhood's small-business character.

After the days of the Woodland Theatre, that building at 1011 Woodland Street was re-shaped and made into the Woodland Sound Studios. (By now, the broad term "Music Row" had spread to other areas of the city. It was not confined to that initial area of 16th Avenue, South.)

Those fine Woodland Sound Studios of notable recordings were operated by Glenn Snoddy who was one of the outstanding recording engineers in Nashville. He built these studios which had features some others didn't have. Glenn's touch put the studios on the map.

The studios' mikes and giant boards had made recordings by the likes of Johnny Cash, Barbara Mandrell, the Oak Ridge Boys, Conway Twitty, Loretta Lynn, and, some younger people will remember that Kansas recorded there.

From those who know more about the group Kansas, I have learned that the group recorded "Dust in the Wind" at the studio. That song was released on Kansas' 1977 *Point of No Return* album which sold more than 3 million records.

At one time, I taught a night music business class at McGavock High School for adults and continuing education students. During the course, I took my students on a number of field trips to publishing houses and recording studios.

I remember taking the students to one recording studio where we learned that the engineers had a tape of Elvis Presley singing songs which had never been released. That night, my students and I got to hear the whole tape of Elvis Presley before it was offered to the world.

Another time I got permission from Glenn Snoddy to take my students on a field trip to the Woodland Sound Studios and observe a recording session. The students got to see the studio, observe the operations, and watch a producer and musicians at work.

In 2002, it was reported that two musicians, Gillian Welch and David Rawlings, would buy the old Woodland Sound Studios, and would use the 11,000 plus square-feet area to record for their own label, Acony Records. The surrounding businesses were happy to hear that the space would be placed in use again.

———•———

The first recording company in Nashville was the old Castle Recording Studio located in the Tulane Hotel which was at the corner of Eighth Avenue, North and Church Street across from the Paramount Theatre. I learned through my good musician friend since the 1940s, Harold Bradley, who was the brother of Owen Bradley, what the first recording session was at the old Castle Studio. It was a commercial for Harold L.

Shyer Jewelers. You remember Harold: "If you don't know diamonds, know your jeweler. And, if Harold says it's so, it's so!"

Tulane Hotel

Playing at Castle on that commercial were Owen Bradley playing piano, drummer Farris Coursey, bass player George Cooper, singer Snooky Lanson, and Harold Bradley playing guitar. Harold is probably the most recorded guitarist in Nashville. Presently, he also serves as president of the Nashville Association of Musicians. By the way, a lovely lady by the name of Hank Fort wrote that commercial. You may remember that Hank Fort wrote the song "I Didn't Know the Gun Was Loaded."

I remember a lot about the beginnings of the music industry in Music City USA. For instance, in the late 1940s, Pee Wee King and Redd Stewart of the Golden West Cowboys were about ready to accept fifty dollars for a song which they had written, and that is not much money for a song that might become a hit.

There was a songwriter in Nashville at the time named Fred Rose. Fred and Roy Acuff started a new publishing company. Fred asked Pee Wee King and Redd Stewart, "Would you let Acuff-Rose publish your song on a regular, standard royalty basis?" They said that they would.

You know the rest of the story. The song "Tennessee Waltz" became the first song after World War II to sell a million copies of sheet music, and was a million dollar seller for pop singer Patti Page. It has been reported that various versions of "Tennessee Waltz" have reached sales of six million copies.

That contract for the song paid a lot better than fifty dollars, thanks to honest and professionals Fred Rose and Roy Acuff.

I might place the music recorded on Music Row in Nashville over the years in three different categories—three different eras of musical style.

The old country and western music was capitalized on by the *Grand Ole Opry*. Country music was Uncle Jimmy Thompson, Uncle Dave Macon, Humphrey Bate's Possum Hunters, Paul Warmack and his Gully Jumpers, Sam and Kirk McGee, Roy Acuff, Bill Monroe, Hank Williams, Marty Robbins, Ernest Tubb, Red Foley, and we could go on and list a hundred more.

Chet Atkins and Owen Bradley came on the scene and developed the recording industry to new heights. Guitarist Chet Atkins could play different styles of music including jazz. Owen Bradley was primarily a dance band musician playing trombone and piano in the WSM radio staff orchestra.

In order to boost record sales, musicians began wanting

to do different things. I guess they recorded the songs that they personally liked. The music became more of a pop nature with a country flavor which I personally liked.

For instance, we can name Marty Robbins' 1956 "Singin' the Blues," Sonny James did "Young Love," and Ferlin Husky recorded "Gone." Jim Reeves did "He'll Have to Go."

Some more hits of this type were Patsy Cline singing "I Fall to Pieces," Eddy Arnold with his "Make the World Go Away," and Brenda Lee recording "Crazy."

Roger Miller did "Little Green Apples," and "King of the Road." Bill and Dottie West wrote "Here Comes My Baby Back Again," and Ray Price had "For the Good Times." Skeeter Davis had a big hit with Art Kent's song, "The End of the World." Art Kent sang in my church choir in the 1970s when I was the choir director at Calvary United Methodist Church on Hillsboro Road.

Some other "Nashville Sound" products included Jimmy Dean's "Big Bad John," and Don Gibson's doubled sided 1958 single "Oh, Lonesome Me" and "I Can't Stop Loving You."

Any one of these songs mentioned could have been played by a Big Band of the forties and fifties, but here they were formatted with the "Nashville Sound."

I guess we could describe the "Nashville Sound" by saying the song material still had a deeply emotional, country feeling with the artist expressing these values. The accompaniment was the usual country rhythm section of guitars plus drums were used as well as a Floyd Cramer type piano. Horns were used as sweetener. A string section played mostly chord progressions, and back-up singers were used such as The Jordanaires and the Anita Kerr Singers. Voila! The "Nashville Sound."

Today, many of the young artists are recording what I

50

would call pop-country or even pop-rock. I am sure this is an over-simplification of the three eras of musical style recorded on Music Row.

Owen Bradley at one time had a studio over in Hillsboro Village. It was up an alley off of 21st Avenue, South, not far from Acklen Avenue. I remember playing in Owen Bradley's Orchestra for a rehearsal in that studio one night.

After moving the studio out, that location became Acme School Supply Company for a time, and is presently an art store.

Owen and his brother, Harold Bradley, bought an old home on 16th Avenue, South, and built a Quonset hut type structure as a recording studio around or within that old house.

If I am not mistaken, that old house was where my elderly aunt and my cousin lived on 16th Avenue when my family used to visit them. It was long after the death of my aunt and cousin that Owen and Harold Bradley developed the Quonset hut recording studio.

Later, the Bradleys sold the recording studio to CBS Records which evolved into Sony Records which stands at that location today on 16th Avenue, South.

Music Row is something that has physically changed from year to year. I can't be displeased, because some great things have been done in that area.

You should drive over there sometime and look around. It will not be like you remember the area from a few years back. Also, in a month or so, drive back over there again. It will not be the same then either!

Remembering Old Hume-Fogg High School

Nashville's first public school was Hume School, built in 1855 on Broadway between our present Seventh and Eighth Avenues, and named for Alfred Hume, the first Superintendent of Schools in Nashville.

In 1874, Fogg School was built beside Hume School and named for Francis Fogg, the first president of the Nashville School Board. Both Hume and Fogg are buried in Nashville's Old City Cemetery at Fourth Avenue, South and Oak Street.

Both schools were torn down in 1910, and Hume-Fogg High School was built at that location, and still stands today on Broadway between Seventh and Eighth Avenues downtown.

My sister, Elva Griffin, who is seven years older than I, was cleaning out some things from drawers and closets at her home. She ran across a folder which contained information that she received when attending her 55th reunion of the class of 1935 from Hume-Fogg High School.

I attended Hume-Fogg for one year. After that 1939-1940 school year, I transferred to the new West End High School at Bowling and West End Avenues. Because of my knowledge and interest in the old Hume-Fogg, I enjoyed looking over my sister's folder of materials.

There were page excerpts from the old Hume-Fogg student published, weekly newspaper called *The Tatler*. Also, there were some very interesting pages from another Hume-Fogg High School publication which was named *The Echo*. Those two names will be very familiar to all of you old Hume-Fogg graduates.

In fact, all of you readers will remember some of the things which I saw on those pages that should spark a glimmer of nostalgic happiness.

All of us used to go to movies downtown, and end up for a delicious ice cream delight at Candyland which stood at the corner of Seventh Avenue and Church Street right across the street from Castner-Knott Dry Goods Company.

In this particular issue of Hume-Fogg's 1935 newspaper, the complete menu was listed from Candyland. For instance, a large serving of ice cream in those well-remembered silver bowls cost ten cents. You could get either vanilla, chocolate, caramel pecan, or English toffee.

Ice cream sodas and sundaes cost fifteen cents. Nut sundaes were twenty cents. A limeade was ten cents, and a limeade freeze was fifteen cents.

I remember that Sonia, my wife, loved the marshmallow nut sundae with those little chocolate spriggles on top. It cost twenty cents. For myself, I was strictly a chocolate soda man.

Sometimes many of us didn't have twenty cents. So, the high school newspaper often had a coupon we could clip out which read: "This ticket and five cents entitles you to a JUMBO ice cream sandwich at Woolworth."

On a page from the March 23, 1934 issue of *The Tatler*, under a column called "City News," I found this item: "The Knickerbocker Theatre celebrated its 18th anniversary last Friday with a bang. The picture, *Wonder Bar*, one of the best musicals of the year, drew crowds every day."

If my math is correct, and the 18th anniversary was observed in 1934, then the Knickerbocker Theatre must have opened in 1916. I can recall that just a few years ago, I could stand at the big picture-window at the now demolished Church Street Center on Church Street, and looking up Capitol Boulevard, I could still see the name "Knickerbocker" painted on the side of the building.

On that same page from the 1934 Hume-Fogg publication, there was an ad for Loew's Theatre which advertised their showing of *Catherine the Great* starring Douglas Fairbanks, Jr. and Elizabeth Bergner. By the way, Douglas Fairbanks, Jr. passed away not too long ago on Sunday, May 7, 2000 at the age of 90. He along with his great acting father brought wonderful entertainment happiness to many lives.

In this same issue of Hume-Fogg's *The Tatler*, there were many statements about the R. O. T. C. (Reserved Officer's Training Corps.) I was in the ROTC for the one year that I attended Hume-Fogg. Each morning we had to march down to the old Hay Market between Third and Fourth Avenues where there was enough space to drill.

Under a column called "Alumni News," I saw this item: "Jack Harris, graduate of the class of '29, is an announcer over WSM."

Yes, Jack Harris was a fine announcer whom all of us heard, and he later became the president of WSM radio before moving to Texas.

There was a full-page advertisement about the up-coming Air Show to open the Municipal Airport in 1937. An adult's ticket cost 40 cents. Seems to me that was a little expensive back in 1937. The article mentioned R. W. "Dick" Jones who was the WPA Chief Engineer in charge of airport construction in Tennessee, Colonel Harry S. Berry who was the Tennessee WPA administrator, and Hilary Howse who was the mayor of Nashville.

On a page from the March, 1935, issue of *The Echo*, I saw ads for Life & Casualty Insurance Company, Stumb's Ice Cream, and Ambrose Printing Company.

The old Wagon Wheel dinner club, which was located roughly where highways 100 and 70 divide, was a little before my time, but I enjoyed reading where the up-coming attractions were going to be Jan Garber and His Orchestra, Vincent Lopez and His Orchestra, and Ozzie Nelson and His Orchestra featuring Harriett Hilliard.

Also, there was an ad for the Wagon Wheel which featured a hamburger with lettuce and tomato on a bun for 15 cents, steak with lettuce and tomato on a bun for 25 cents, and a club sandwich for 50 cents. You could get ham or bacon and eggs for 25 cents. The last line of the ad read: "Please write your own order and pay when served."

I remember that my sister and her boy friend double-dated with Dorothy Dean Loser and her boy friend when they attended the Wagon Wheel. Fats Waller and His Orchestra was playing there at the time.

Dorothy Dean Loser was at our house a lot. She was the daughter of J. Carlton Loser who served many years as our District Attorney, and later served as our U. S. Congressman.

My sister said she presumed the name Wagon Wheel was given to the dinner club because it was decorated in a rustic motif.

Many great bands of the time played there. I wish I could have played the Wagon Wheel, but I never did. Also, I wish I could still go and hear some of those great bands today.

Athens of the South

When I was growing up, Nashville was always referred to as "The Athens of the South." It was many years later that Nashville became "Music City USA." Of course, we are happy to have both titles.

The reference to Nashville as "The Athens of the South" goes way back. Philip Lindsley, who was the chancellor of the old University of Nashville from 1824 until 1855, used the identity for Nashville as "Athens of the West." He probably was referring to the political role, as well as to education and culture of our city. However, the term "Athens of the South" became official when Tennessee Governor Bob Taylor used it in his speech at the opening of the Tennessee Centennial Exposition in 1897.

When someone asks you why we are known as "The Athens of the South," what do you tell them? I usually try to answer the question quickly by saying, "Because of our extensive classical Greek architecture and cultural opportunities. We have the only exact replica of the Parthenon which stood in Athens, Greece, and we have many colleges and universities here."

Actually, we could go on and say much more. There are many examples of Greek revival architecture in Nashville. Our Tennessee State Capitol building takes on the attitude of an Ionic Temple. It is a good example of Greek revival architecture.

On the north and south sides of the Capitol there are

eight Ionic columns, and six each on the east and west sides, making a total of twenty-eight. The tower is supported by eight columns of pure Corinthian style.

The Belle Meade Plantation Mansion is Greek revival displaying its six columns at the very front of the building, and Acklen Hall at Belmont University gives us examples of Corinthian columns.

There are the beautiful columns at the Hermitage, former home of President Andrew Jackson. The Greek revival style is carried throughout the Hermitage mansion.

Stately pillars also stand at Tulip Grove.

Speaking of columns, how about the War Memorial Building? That structure is an example of Greek revival architecture. Also, many church buildings reflect this classical style including Saint Mary's Catholic Church, Downtown Presbyterian Church, Belmont United Methodist Church, Westminster Presbyterian Church, and others.

The Peabody College campus offers many examples of classical architecture such as the old Social-Religious Building which is now named the Vanderbilt Wyatt Center.

Our new Nashville Public Library downtown acknowledges the classical tradition of our city's public architecture, such as the State Capitol and the Parthenon. And, the new Schermerhorn Symphony Hall under construction in downtown Nashville will reflect this classical attitude.

Even in the suburbs of Nashville, there are private homes which establish the values of permanence and stability which are upheld by the use of columns and classical Greek architecture.

Not to be overlooked is the place of literature, music, and the arts which have played a role from the early years of Nashville's history.

Of course, Nashville has the only exact-size replica of the Parthenon which was a Greek Temple sitting atop the Acropolis in ancient Athens, Greece.

Our Parthenon was originally built as a temporary structure to serve as the center attraction for our Centennial Exposition which was staged in 1897 (one year after our real centennial date of 1896) in West Side Park off of West End Avenue. That park was later re-named Centennial Park.

The Parthenon was built of wood, plaster, and stucco. The other structures in the park were torn down after the centennial celebration. The people of Nashville wanted to keep the Parthenon. Of course, it would soon deteriorate to nothing being just a temporary building. So, the Parthenon was structured permanently with reinforced concrete. The interior of the building was completed in 1925 and the exterior in 1931.

The Parthenon

Today, the Parthenon houses a re-creation by Nashville sculptor Alan LeQuire of Pheidias's original monumental statue of Athena Parthenos. This Nashville Athena, approximately forty-two feet tall, was unveiled in 1990. Athena was the mythical goddess of wisdom and the arts. Regardless of the religious beliefs of the time, which we do not embrace, it is still part of history, and this statue in our Parthenon is the tallest indoor statue in the western world.

When sculptor Alan LeQuire was working on this project, I was working with my sister and brother-in-law who owned Griffin Supply Company in Nashville. We would often see Alan when he came into the store to purchase certain art materials.

Welcome to The Athens of the South.

Nashville Businesses Date Way Back

Some of the old Nashville businesses are still with us, but many are institutions of our great past. I was shocked to learn the dates as to when many of the businesses first came into existence.

Weinstein's came into existence in 1890. You should know Davitt's which came in 1897. All photographic buffs know Dury's which came in 1882.

Standard Candy Company (1902) is a company which gives me great memories from my youth. Mr. Scobey Rogers was the bookkeeper at Standard for a long time. I knew him through his work in the Boy Scouts as well as through his son, Scobey Rogers, Jr. That whole family was an inspiration.

You are familiar with Baird Electric Company (1897), H. Brown & Company (1902), and Life & Casualty Insurance Company (1903). Joy Floral Company was around in 1877, and Geny's Floral date is 1882.

I can remember my family shopping at Phillips & Buttorff. That company came into existence in 1858 which was before the Civil War.

Gray & Dudley came in 1862. When I was a kid, we used to go to the old baseball diamonds across from Centennial Park, and see various teams play which were sponsored by Nashville businesses. I remember the Gray & Dudley baseball team.

The old Centennial Park baseball diamonds were located on 25th Avenue, North where today sits the Centennial SportsPlex.

As a kid out of school enjoying the hot summers, I remember the big concession stand which sat right behind the home plate screen on the corner of 25th Avenue, North and Brandau Place. Also, back in those days, we could buy a cold drink, Popsicle, popcorn, peanuts, or ice cream without it costing us an arm and a leg!

You remember B. H. Stief Jewelry Company. It was a fine jewelry store downtown on Sixth Avenue when I remember it. The company came into existence in 1858.

How about printing companies? The oldest is Marshall and Bruce opening October 25, 1865, on old Deaderick Street which Alfred Leland Crabb described as "a lane usually either muddy or dusty." Ambrose Printing also came to Nashville in 1865.

Cumberland Manufacturing Company came in 1898. One of my sister's first jobs out of junior college was with that company when it was located in Cummings Station.

Hatch Show Print was organized in 1879, and is still a tourist attraction today through its fine posters.

May Hosiery Mill came around in 1863, the Methodist Publishing House in 1856, and Nashville Tent & Awning in 1884.

Union Ice Cream Company organized in 1892. Rock City Ice Cream Company came into existence in 1897.

I'll surely have to mention Cain-Sloan Company (1903) and Castner-Knott Dry Goods Company (1899) where my wife, Sonia, spent 14 years in sales after retiring as a school teacher and a stay-at-home Mom.

Some people say that Harvey's really dates back to Lebeck Brothers department store which came into existence in 1874. However, the true Harvey's Department Store appeared in the early 1940s. Loveman, Berger & Teitlebaum was here in 1862.

I am reminded of another Loveman. Loveman Lumber & Box Company came into existence in 1865. Maurice Loveman, who continued the business, and his dear wife were friends of ours. Maurice played flute, and could be seen almost anywhere fine music was being played. The Lovemans played a great part in supporting not only our present Nashville Symphony Orchestra which was established in 1946, but also an earlier symphony orchestra directed by Maestro F. Arthur Henkle.

Back in the 1920s, Conductor Henkle led 62 of Nashville's own musicians in the first concert of this Nashville Symphony Orchestra on the stage of the old Princess Theatre located on Church Street.

Some of you may remember the names of the officers of that old Nashville Symphony Society. George Pullen Jackson was the president, and Mrs. Milton Cook was the vice-president. Her husband, Milton Cook, was the roving music teacher in the public schools when I was in elementary school. Maurice Loveman was the secretary-treasurer of the Symphony Society.

The wonderful, old Frank School of Music arrived on the Nashville scene in 1907 and was around until the early 1950s. Leon Frank, a piano prodigy, began the school and saw it grow to enroll many students who were taught by a distinguished music faculty including Lawrence Goodman, a leading pianist in Nashville. At one time there were 10 piano teachers on the faculty.

Milton Cook, who was the Director of Music for the Nashville public schools and the choir director of the First Presbyterian Church downtown, had great credentials in voice training after studying with some of the greatest voice teachers in London, Paris and Berlin. Ursula McCampbell headed the violin department. Charles Davis was a director in the school's department of orchestral and band instruments.

A fine old name in Nashville's history is Keith-Simmons Company which arrived in 1898. Ladies will remember Tinsleys. They came on the scene first in 1902.

Petway-Reavis on Church Street is still here. I remember the last hat I bought was at Petway-Reavis. I used to wear hats. As a young man, I was cool before cool became popular!

At one time, Broadway was a location where shoppers traveled to buy their dining room tables and bedroom suites. Harley-Holt was started in 1904 by Edwin L. Holt. Later, his grandson, Ed Holt, took over the business. Then, Ed's daughter, Marion Wilmoth, ran the business on Broadway.

After 99 years, Harley-Holt closed its doors in 2003. Ed Holt said that the company was doing well until the year 2000. Then, business began to fall off. Furniture delivery to and from the store became a big problem. Marion, as a fourth generation Holt, said that she wanted to continue in furniture, but not at the old Broadway location.

I haven't listed every company, of course, but I hope many of these names will kindle a spark of nostalgic happiness in your life, as surely they do in mine.

———— • ————

I remember Lower Broad as living three contrasting lives. All of the happenings were done with the observing eyes of various Nashville historic groups fighting for Nashville and its culture.

When I was a kid, Lower Broad meant shopping at furniture stores, and citizens working their finances at a number of banks.

In phase two, I remember Lower Broad as a run-down area. Many good businesses moved out. X-rated movies and peep shows were locating there along with some good businesses who were still trying to hold on to decent culture in the area.

The third phase saw peep shows and sex shops moving out. We saw the Convention Center operating in the area. Restaurants went in. Merchants Hotel had been renovated. Second Avenue was developed. Many Nashvillians made renovated locations on Second Avenue as their permanent residences.

Unfortunately, we saw at least one tragedy occur. For many years at 101 Broadway, we saw and were inspired by the nostalgic flavor of our Tennessee farmers. For 60 years we saw the historic three-story building with the painted red-and-white checkerboards. Acme Farm Supply store on the corner of First Avenue and Broadway seemed to brave many storms. But, finally, in 1999, it was gone!

The Acme Company was over 90 years old. The store opened in 1907 down on the City Square. It was called Acme Stock and Poultry Company. The name was later changed to Acme Feed and Grain. You may remember when it was named Acme Feed and Hatchery, and moved to lower Broadway in the early 1940s.

In more recent days, one could stand inside at the front window of Acme Farm Supply and see the block-long guitar painted across the side of the Hard Rock Café across the street. Of course, until just a few years ago, the Hard Rock Café building was the home of Phillips and Quarles Hardware store.

We shall always remember the old wooden floors at Acme Farm Supply where farmers came in to buy their farm supplies and seed for planting. Many times one could enjoy seeing the hundreds of baby chicks hatched there in an incubator.

Sorrowfully, if you want to buy some Purina dog food today, you will have to go somewhere else. Acme Farm Supply at First Avenue and Broadway is no more.

Ma Moore's Mission

Tim H. Moore was my wife's grandfather. Pa Moore, as Sonia called him, was part owner of Moore & Hadley Buggy and Harness Company in Nashville back during the beginning of the twentieth century. Sonia's grandparents were religious people who had a desire to act as the Lord's servants.

Sonia's grandmother, Fannie Moore, being the wife of Tim H. Moore was blessed in having enough money to express her actions within her Christian faith. Ma Moore, as Sonia knew her, felt that the Lord wanted her to help the underprivileged in Nashville. Ma Moore said, "God has put that on my heart."

Ma Moore traveled the streets of Nashville back during the first decade of the 1900s in her own horse-drawn buggy. Ma Moore looked for girls who were under-privileged or at the age when they might get into trouble. Some girls had no strong family back-up to help them.

Ma Moore's philosophy read: "How much easier to save a girl to a life of purity than to rescue one from a life of sin."

Ma Moore went around Nashville in her side-curtained adorned black buggy pulled by her horse named Prince. Ma even went down to the shacks on the river banks to find young girls she might could help. She talked to the parents to encourage them to let her take the girls into her home where she would feed, clothe, house, and give the girls an education. Ma Moore called it a home. She never referred to it as an orphanage.

And, yes, Fannie Moore bought a home in East Nashville for this purpose which she would call her Pentecostal Mission

Training Home. It was the old Driver home located at the end of McFerrin Street near West Greenwood Avenue. That area today is where Ellington Parkway passes through.

At the home, Ma taught the girls housekeeping, cooking, sewing, and various other skills. She employed a school teacher to teach the girls to read, write, use math, and actually give them an education.

Ma Moore's daughter, Adaline, who was Sonia's mother, taught the girls music. Ma Moore's other daughter, Sonia's Aunt Ruth, taught the girls art appreciation, drawing and painting.

People from all around heard about this new training home in Nashville, and they would ask if Ma would be able to take their daughter. The school started with a few girls, but it began to expand until Ma had quite a few girls enrolled. Each older girl was assigned a younger girl to care for.

In 1908, Ma Moore had a large, one-room school building built adjoining the home. The home itself had 14 rooms.

Pentecostal Mission Training Home

Water was plentiful from two large tanks. The girls tended cows and chickens on the grounds. Every two weeks, the girls would rotate their jobs and chores.

The school included the first grade through the eighth grade. The home and school soon grew to 35 girls enrolled. Present family members still remember much about the home. Miss Nettie Ogden was hired as the matron, and Miss Pearl Paul served as assistant matron. Ma Moore continued her home until around 1917. More than 200 girls passed through the school at some time.

As time continued, the girls grew up. Some stayed in the home and worked just like family members, some others married and started their own families, some got jobs as secretaries, receptionists, or some other employment.

Since I have known my wife, Sonia, for more than 50 years, I had the pleasure of personally knowing three of these "girls" as they were referred to by some family members. Sonia and the younger family members always referred to them as "aunts." Of course, there was no biological relation at all to the girls in the home. It was a family that Ma Moore developed through being the Lord's servant.

The three that I knew were Aunt Ozella, Aunt Nelle, and Aunt Gladys. Of course, they were older than Sonia and I. They were the age of Sonia's mother.

Aunt Ozella went into a good marriage and reared a wonderful daughter whom I personally knew, also.

Aunt Nelle went on to a business college, and developed the necessary office skills to become Pa Moore's secretary in his business. Later, Nelle married a wealthy man from Birmingham. They had one son and one daughter. I met Nelle's husband once as well as their son who went into real estate.

Aunt Gladys was the one I knew best. She married and had a daughter. Aunt Gladys was around us more than any of the others. In fact, when Sonia, our son Jeff, and I lived in Evansville, Indiana while I was teaching at Evansville College, our wonderful daughter was born.

Aunt Gladys' husband had died, and I remember that she said she would be glad to come to Evansville and stay with us for a week to cook and help Sonia with the new baby.

After our daughter, Lee Anne, was born, I got a phone call from Aunt Gladys. She said to meet her just after she crossed the Ohio River between Kentucky and Indiana so she could follow me on out to our home in Evansville. Sure enough, Jeff and I sat there, and here came Aunt Gladys puttering up in her old, but faithful, 1962 Chevrolet.

Back in those days, a new mother stayed in the hospital for exactly one full week. So, when Sonia and the baby came home, Aunt Gladys was there to cook some of the most fabulous meals you could imagine. Sonia was observing how these meals were being cooked, as well as having the blessing of Aunt Gladys' helping hand with the new baby.

I don't guess too many people know about Ma Moore's old Pentecostal Mission Training Home in East Nashville back during the early years of the 1900s. But, now, you know about it.

The title of this story could be "From River Shanties to Honorable Citizens," and, it would be the truth!

One family member recently volunteered telling us what Ma Moore's favorite Bible verse was. It was Ecclesiastes 11:1:

"Cast thy bread upon the waters: for thou shalt find it after many days." (King James Version)

Nashville's First Skyscraper

I have wonderful memories of the old Third National Bank Building downtown at the corner of Fourth Avenue, North and Church Street. The building is still there, and the twelve-story structure was really Nashville's first "sky-scraper" built in 1905. The reason that the building looks much younger today is because in 1936 the Third National Bank was growing and needed more space. So, the bank bought the building and the vacant lot behind it to make room for expansion. The bank built a twelve-story addition to the original building and with a more modern facade. Today, the building looks newer because of that. But, the old original building was built in 1905. The old, still-standing Stahlman Building was our second "sky-scraper" completed in 1906.

One day I decided to walk into this old Third National Bank building and look around. I knew that my mind would spin with such a spirit of nostalgia. Sure enough, it brought a goose bump on my back big enough to hang my hat on.

In 1941, when I was a musician playing at WLAC radio atop that grand, old building, it was surrounded by the Noel Hotel on one corner, the historic Maxwell House Hotel on another corner, and some low-standing buildings on the fourth corner. On that corner, the thirty-one-story L & C (Life and Casualty) Tower, which is there now, was not built until 1957.

It dawned on me that the old Third National Building was constructed in the year 1905. That means that in 2005, the building will celebrate its 100th anniversary. I pray that it makes it!

In 1905, the building was named the First National Bank Building. Later, the building became the Independent Life Insurance Company Building. Then, finally it became the Third National Bank Building when I rode the elevators up to the twelfth floor and stepped out into the WLAC radio reception lobby and studios.

It was in 1968 when a financial institution, J. C. Bradford Company, moved into the building and was re-named the J. C. Bradford Company Building.

When J. C. Bradford moved out after about 18 years, the great, old building sat empty for about 11 years, from 1986 until 1997. I was frightened that the good building would be torn down to make room for another parking lot. Not so! Plans moved toward renovating the building and becoming a Courtyard by Marriott Hotel which it is today.

While looking around on the twelfth floor of the hotel that day I visited, my mind visualized every part of old WLAC radio station. The reception desk stood there at the elevators. If you walked down the hall to the right side, you would find the many offices of WLAC which included announcers, secretaries, copy writers, traffic manager, program director, producers, and others. The station manager's office was occupied by Mr. F. C. Sowell. He was a fine announcer, too.

At that time, the head of the station was Mr. Truman Ward. You should be interested in knowing that Mr. Ward's secretary was Bellevue's Sara Elizabeth Wilhite. She is a reader of the *Westview* Newspaper, and she called me on the phone one day after I had written a column about WLAC radio. Both of us enjoyed reminiscing.

The announcers at WLAC when I was playing there in

1941 were Paul Oliphant, Herman Grizzard, Charlie Roberts, Tim Sanders, and Charles Chumley. All of them were very fine announcers with those required beautiful, pear-shaped tones which went out over the airwaves. I remember an outstanding radio engineer who worked for many years at WLAC by the name of Allen Dunkerley.

As I stood there that day visiting the hotel with my mind whirling, I could visualize seeing Studio B where the announcers worked when on the air. I visualized Studio C where I auditioned back in 1941. I especially visualized the great Studio A where the studio orchestra was set up on risers, the giant Kilgen pipe organ which Mary Elizabeth Hicks played during her 28 years on the musical staff, and other musical instruments such as the piano, solo vox, nova chord, and drum-set.

Sorrowfully, Mary Elizabeth Hicks passed away in July of 2004. I am thankful for the nice telephone conversations we had prior to her passing.

Believe me, as I stood there, I almost could hear the station-break and then the theme of *Ranch House Melodies* with Curly, Red and Shorty. I could almost hear Mary Elizabeth Hicks at the organ, and Fred Murff at the piano. I could almost hear Texas Daisy as she played her guitar and sang on morning shows. I could think of hearing Big Jeff and His Radio Playboys. They did a show following my *Ranch House Melodies*. Big Jeff Bess was married to Tootsie Bess who owned and operated Tootsie's Orchid Lounge out behind the Grand Ole Opry when it was at the Ryman Auditorium.

You probably remember when radio stations presented *The Man on the Street* shows. Herman Grizzard used to go with his engineer up to the Arcade at Fourth Avenue and interview a crowd of people waiting there. If they could answer a certain question following their interview, they would receive a prize such as theatre tickets.

I stood there in the old building that day and thought about the CBS program called *The Garden Gate* which originated at WLAC in Nashville featuring "The Old Dirt Dobber" with Paul Oliphant as his announcer.

Finally, it was time to take the elevator back down to the first floor and walk out onto the streets of my beloved Nashville. When I did, I saw the Noel Hotel building, but it was not the Noel Hotel. The corner with the huge Sun Trust Bank Building stood where the old Maxwell House Hotel used to stand.

If you saw me that day, you may have seen some tears well up in my eyes. That's O. K. I'm an old man, and I couldn't help it.

Railroading in Nashville

From my childhood, I have had a great love for trains. My father was a railroader, and our family rode trains around America on passes which employees were given.

I proudly own a brake stick which was used by a railroad brakeman. The brakeman would go on top of the old freight cars to bring them to a stop. After a car was sent off of "the hump" in the yard, the brakeman would ride the car to its designated track location and stop it by turning the brake wheel with his very hard, oak brake stick.

I have a lantern which was used by railroaders to give signals in the yards. Later, of course, radios came into use between the brakeman, switchman, foreman, fireman, and the engineer.

Do you remember when freight trains had a red caboose as the last car where the train crew stayed on trips?

Do you remember seeing the New Shops? Do you know where the "round house" was located? It was on Charlotte Avenue around Twenty-Sixth Avenue North not too far from Centennial Park. The round house had several tracks leading into it at different angles so cars and engines could be brought in there for maintenance work.

Do you remember the old Dixie Flyer passenger train, which my family rode many times between Nashville and Chattanooga? Do you remember the Pan American, which went south from Nashville and on to Birmingham and New Orleans?

Each afternoon WSM radio cut-in on the scheduled program to let us hear the train whistle of the Pan American as it passed near their radio tower as the announcer would tell us. Monday through Friday, the scheduled WSM program was a record show called *On the Bandstand.* A record show was unique then, because most of the musical shows on WSM were performed by their live staff orchestra.

Did you ride the trains, sleep in a Pullman car, and eat in the dining car? If so, you remember the efficient porters dressed in their white jackets who served passengers in the sleeping cars.

You remember the immaculately dressed waiters serving meals in the dining car. Entering the diner back in the old days was like entering a restaurant in the Waldorf-Astoria due to its exquisite service and dining car elegance.

Do you remember the dining car steward coming through the coaches sounding chimes announcing first, second, and the last call to dinner?

Do you remember the Humming Bird passenger train? And, do you remember when the last remaining passenger train through Nashville, Amtrax Floridian, was discontinued?

My father worked for the railroad as a foreman in the Radnor Yard as well as the yard at Union Station. In the eyes of a small child, Radnor Yard seemed to be very large in the area south of Nashville off of Franklin Road. Radnor Yard, in a different format, is still there today.

You can't think of the Radnor Yard without thinking about Radnor Lake. Back in the old days, the 85-acre Radnor Lake off of Otter Creek Road was owned by the L & N (Louisville and Nashville) Railroad Company. The man-made lake served as a water supply for the steam engines operating at the nearby Radnor Railroad Yard as well as for the livestock at its property.

Do you remember that the conductor on passenger trains used to walk through the coaches and call out the names of the stations?

Do you know that the conductor on the passenger train from Nashville to Memphis called out Bellevue and Pegram, and in the old days, I heard the conductor once call out "Vaughan's Gap." The train stopped at Vaughan's Gap to either let someone off or take on a passenger. How I would love to see some of those old days again.

I enjoy thinking about trains. They were a big part of my life.

———————•———————

The old Tennessee Central Railroad played a vital part in the growth of the city of Nashville. The old TC Depot was on First Avenue at the foot of Broadway near the Cumberland River. Today, there are tracks which still run beside the river.

The old Tennessee Central tracks surrounded many areas of Nashville's old city limits. The TC tracks were the city's boundary on the old Lebanon Road. Where I grew up, the TC tracks crossed Belmont Boulevard near Gale Lane which at that time was the boundary of the old city limits of Nashville. Interstate 440 cuts through that area now.

The Tennessee Central Railroad was chartered in 1893 by a Nashville attorney by the name of Jere Baxter. He hoped to give competition to the already established L & N Railroad and the N C & St. L Railroad.

After the death of Jere Baxter, he was honored by having a full length statue cast in bronze and displayed on a large base. For a long time, this statue stood at the junction of Broadway and West End Avenue.

Later, the statue was moved to the front of Jere Baxter Elementary School at the corner of Gallatin Road and Hart Lane in East Nashville. The statue stood there for many years.

After the new Jere Baxter School was built, the statue was moved to the front of the new school where it stands today.

The new Jere Baxter Middle School is located on out Hart Lane going from Gallatin Road and across Ellington Parkway. The school sits up on a hill, and this very distinguished statue of Jere Baxter and the monument have an honored place right by the flagpole before the main entrance of the school.

Railroads used to play quite an important role in the life and progress of our city.

There used to be a train depot in West Nashville serving the Tennessee Central Railroad. The TC rail had been extended to the community which made connections as far north as Hopkinsville, Kentucky and as far east as Harriman, Tennessee.

When the railroad company became very much in debt, Jere Baxter went to St. Louis hopefully to get some financial aid from friends. He was successful. Mr. Jacob Craig Van Blarcom, president of the National Bank of Commerce, was the central figure in saving the railroad.

Tennessee Central Railroad engine

After Jere Baxter died, Mr. Van Blarcom became the new president of the railroad. When the new depot was built in West Nashville, it was named for Mr. Van Blarcom. The depot was known as Van Blarcom Station. It was located in a triangle at present Thirty-first and Charlotte Avenues.

In October of 1927, Governor Austin Peay's body was placed on a train at Van Blarcom Station on its way to Clarksville, Tennessee for burial in Greenwood Cemetery.

Years ago, we were able to board the old Broadway Dinner Train for a thirty-five mile, roundtrip excursion to Old Hickory, TN while eating a served dinner in a dining car of the old train days. Sorrowfully, the old Broadway Dinner Train made its last run in July of 1999.

Still, a group of train enthusiasts meets regularly and plan excursions to Lebanon, Watertown, Cookeville, and other locations. That Excursion Train also serves meals on certain trips. They use rebuilt railroad cars and an engine reminiscent of the great old days of train travel.

The Excursion Train is operated by the Tennessee Central Railway Museum located in the former TC Railway Master Mechanic's office and stores department building at 220 Willow Street.

Hi (Hillard) Brown, a friend of mine dating all the way back to our youth in old Boy Scout Troop 26, told me about his grandfather who worked for the Tennessee Central Railroad.

Hillard's grandfather, Clarence Ollie Brown, was a dispatcher on the TC for more than 50 years. His initials C. O. B. was his signature on the telegraph; thus, he was known from Hopkinsville to Harriman Junction as Cob Brown.

Hi told me that his grandfather taught him code at an early age, a fact which he credits winning the Morse Signaling contest at Boy Scout field day one year. Cob knew every switch and siding on the TC.

When Hi was in college at Tennessee Tech, he rode the train back and forth regularly but never had to let his parents know to meet him at the depot. But, his parents always met him, for when Hi would board the train, Mr. Wiggins, the depot clerk at Cookeville, would tap it out on his telegraph "bug" and every station agent on the line would know that Cob's grandson was on Number One.

The Old Grocery Store

Did you live during the time we had grocery stores rather than super markets? When I was a kid, we didn't have the large, modern stores or the sprawling, all-purpose retail stores. Instead of a "greeter" at the door, we would be welcomed by the owner or manager of the store.

I can still remember the smells that enriched my nostrils each time I opened the door to the old grocery store. One could smell spices, fresh bread, fruity scents, and the warm aroma from the wood burning potbelly stove in some cases.

When I was a kid, I had several connections to the old fashioned grocery store.

My cousin, Murray Kennedy, for a time operated a grocery store located at 44th Avenue and Wyoming in West Nashville. I had an uncle who traveled the state of Tennessee for the Quaker Oats Company. He was in and out of grocery stores all day long. Later, he bought a grocery store in South Nashville, and ran it himself. By doing that, he didn't have to travel so much, and could spend more time with his family.

During The Great Depression, my father was laid off in his work with the railroad. He was a foreman in the yard at the Union Station or at the Radnor Yard. Money became a little scarce during that time except when his name would show up on the "extra board" and he would get a day or night's work and draw a little money. So, during that period, my daddy took on a job as butcher at the Tidwell's Grocery on 12th Avenue, South. I remember that his butcher section of the grocery floor was covered with saw dust. In the middle he had a large cutting table with many knives and cleavers hanging around.

There was a small grocery store about a block from where I grew up. If my mother sent me to the grocery to pick up a quart of milk, sack of meal, or some beans, I would simply tell Mr. Harris what I wanted. All of the stock was on shelves around the walls. Mr. Harris would get what I wanted, and write up a grocery ticket for me to take home.

All of my life from about age 6 or 7, I thought the name

H.G. Hill Grocery Store
James Cathey, T.C. Young,
M. Odum (1916)

of the grocery store was the Harris Grocery, and that's what I called it. About 70 years later, I learned from my sister and another eighty-year old neighbor, James Kilgore who is still our friend, that it was the Stephens Grocery. So, I presume Mr. Harris ran the store, and Harris was all I knew.

Of course, some food was grown at home back then. My grandmother had many chickens, and she kept us in supply of eggs. My parents grew asparagus, radishes, potatoes, onions, and other things at our home. We had a fine cherry tree in the backyard. Mother could get a couple of wonderful cherry pies out of that tree each season. Also, we had a great peach tree. We learned early in life that fruit and vegetables were what we needed health wise.

But, unfortunately, for us kids our favorite glassed-in case in the grocery store held the candy. For a few cents, we could get suckers, jelly beans, peppermint candy sticks, jaw breakers, bubble gum, and licorice sticks.

By the way, back in those days, shoplifting was not a concern. There weren't any two-way mirrors or security cameras. Back then, the only deterrent to stealing was our parents and our neighbors, and it worked!

When the automobile became popular, some old grocery stores added a gas pump out front to take advantage of this new product. I remember the old pumps where you could see the gasoline up in the tank at the top. It would go down as you pumped the gas into your car. I can remember when gas was 17 cents a gallon.

Bellevue used to have an old-time grocery store. I am not referring to Wiggin's Market. At one time, a filling station and Wiggin's Market were the only two businesses along a strip of Highway 70 South. A picture of that is in the *History of Bellevue* written by Doug Underwood.

I am talking about the store located at the corner of Bellevue Road and Old Harding Road near the railroad tracks. According to Paula Underwood Winters, editor of the *Westview* Newspaper, it was the T. L. Herrin General Merchandise Store. Also, the Bellevue Post Office was in that building. Elmo Mitchell owned the property, but he leased it to Frank and Dolly Carter around the 1960s, and they operated a store which I remember well. It was the Bellevue Market. I was by there often in the old days. Of course, you may know to our horror that Frank was shot and killed by a robber around the mid-1990s. The building has since been torn down. Dolly is still in Bellevue, and loved by all. Every time I see her, I enjoy a little musical greeting with "Hello Dolly."

Of course, there are many advantages to having a large super market with all of its frills; but, if you can't remember the old fashioned grocery stores, then maybe my description above may help you slightly with the nostalgic spirit which I remember.

The Games We Played

Today, we are bombarded with newspaper and TV ads about the wonderful electrical, mechanical, and high-tech toys such as Nintendo, Play Station, four wheeling Jeep, mini-stereo home theatre system, dual deck 4-head hi-fi stereo VCR, and an 8mm compact view-cam with 3-inch LCD screen which we are supposed to purchase in this day and time when we need to find gifts for a child on a birthday, Christmas, Hanukkah, Kwaanza, graduation, or other celebration.

It wasn't quite like that when some of us came up as children during The Great Depression. All of us kids played outside on a vacant lot, or under a street light after dark. We couldn't pay anything to play.

We played such games as Hide-and-seek; Hopscotch; Mother, May I; London Bridge; Red Rover; Sling the Statue; Charades; Tug-of-war; and Kick the Can. Even with a piece of string, we could tie a "cat's cradle."

None of those games cost us anything. We had never heard the expression, "Batteries not included."

If we had a nickel or a dime, we could really engage in high-priced toys. For a few cents, we could buy a flat cardboard game at the drugstore. We would spend a lot of time trying to make a BB drop into a shallow hole in that piece of cardboard by tilting it this way and that.

Boys would fly a kite. Girls would skip a rope. The girls would enjoy a set of ball-and-jacks. That would keep them busy for hours. The boys would buy or trade a few marbles. You know the kind I mean. Any respectable marble shooter would have a collection of pee-wees, crockers, glasses, toofers, imitations, steelies, and those most cherished agates.

We would draw a circle in the dirt, and shoot marbles. No fee required. However, it seemed like the bigger boys had more strength in their fingers and thumb, and could really shoot those marbles like a cue stick attacking a pool ball, and take all of our marbles when we played "for keeps."

Of course, a rubber ball attached to a paddle gave us real reason to have some contests. Also, the Yo-Yo would become a real skill in loopty-loop, walking the dog, cradle the baby, and around the world.

Then, there were a few of us who were more interested in creativity. It wasn't that hard to make a soap-box racer, or a scooter.

To make a scooter, we would get a board and attach some old roller skates to the bottom for the wheels. Then, with another board nailed on perpendicular to the first board, we had a scooter. We would nail on a smaller piece of wood at the top for a handle to hold on to. Then, we might nail an old tin can on the front to look like a head light.

My greatest love was to find enough old lead pipes to form some railroad tracks. We would take the old, hard, rubber wheels off of a wagon. The curvature of the rims of the wheels would fit perfectly over the lead pipes.

We would start laying our track at the top of the hill. Of course, we had to be very precise in keeping the width of the track the same all the way. This activity alone taught us preciseness, accuracy, dependability, and working as a team. These traits could follow us all through life.

When we had laid enough track, all we had to do was sit the wagon's four wheel rims on the secured track, and down the hill we would go.

Most every kid had an opportunity to get a huge box from the grocery, or retrieve a big box from which a stove or refrigerator had been delivered. That box would become our home away from home. We would cut windows in it, place some things inside like we had a living room and kitchen. It really was something to go into that big box and think we had really built our own house.

How many times have you seen a child get a gift, and then spend most of the time playing with the box that it came in?

Of course, during The Great Depression we couldn't spend all of that money needed for large mechanical toys for which we had no room to store them anyway, and with which we probably would play with for a few minutes and then forget about for a month.

We could yell, "Let's play baseball. Which team wants to be in town?" Or, during football season, we would shout the instruction, "To kick a field goal, you have to get the ball between those two branches in that old, hackberry tree."

We didn't know anything about video games, a mini-stereo home theatre system, or an 8mm slim-cam with 3-inch LCD screen and digital image stabilization. Our happiness was in socializing and making friends for life.

Old Radio Means the *Grand Ole Opry*

Nashville's and WSM's *Grand Ole Opry* is the longest and most successful, continuous radio show in the world. The show has originated from a variety of locations in Nashville over the years, and has gone through massive changes of all kinds. Present day country music is not at all like the original music performed on the Opry.

The first broadcast was in 1925, and believe it or not, I was around. I was only one year old. However, as I grew and listened to radio on Saturday nights, I remember a lot about the OLD *Grand Ole Opry*.

When the Opry first started, people could attend the performances free of charge. The first performances began in old Studio C at the WSM radio studios on the fifth floor of the National Life & Accident Insurance Company building at the corner of Seventh Avenue and Union Street. Studio C at WSM was like a small auditorium. The Opry soon outgrew that location, and found other homes as time went on such as the Belcourt Theatre location in Hillsboro Village which at the time was called the Children's Theatre of Nashville. The Opry played at that location from 1934 until 1936. The Opry performed for some time at the War Memorial Auditorium. The Ryman Auditorium, "the mother church of country music," was the Opry's home from 1943 to 1974.

For a time, the Opry performed from the old Dixie Tabernacle over in East Nashville. I was about twelve years old when my family went over there for the Saturday night, four-hour broadcast over WSM radio.

George D. Hay, "the Solemn Ole Judge," was the master-of-ceremonies. I remember that he would pick up an old steamboat whistle and blow it. The music back then was pure musical Americana. Songs like "Rabbit in a Flea Patch," "Cotton Eye Joe," "Casey Jones," "Sourwood Mountain," and "Greenback Dollar" expressed the pure folk music of this country.

All over the country, people knew the names of the performers on the Opry better than they might recognize their own politicians' names. I remember such names as Uncle Dave Macon who was a banjo player. DeFord Bailey was a harmonica player. I remember Humphrey Bate's Possum Hunters.

Let me tell you a short side story. Many years ago, I sold cancer insurance policies to make some extra money for my family. I sold cancer policies to many musicians including Opry players since I was in the musicians' union with them.

I remember I delivered policies to Tex Ritter, Barbara Mandrell's family, Carl Smith, Sonny James, Don Gibson, and many others.

Dr. Humphrey Bate's daughter was Alcyon Bate Beasley. She also played on the Opry. When I went to her home in East Nashville to deliver her cancer policy, I stayed over an hour. She just couldn't stop talking about the Opry. She had a captive audience in me, and I enjoyed hearing every word of it.

Some other names back in the old, old days of the Opry were Paul Warmack and his Gully-Jumpers, Robert Lunn "the talking blues man," Asher and Little Jimmy, Kirk and Sam McGee, George Wilkerson, Curly Fox, Texas Ruby, Zeke Clements, and the Crook Brothers. Back in those days, the WSM announcer was David Stone.

Then, coming on into a later era, we had such greats as

Roy Acuff and the Smokey Mountain Boys, Bill Monroe and the Bluegrass Boys, Pee Wee King and the Golden West Cowboys, Little Jimmy Dickens, Ernest Tubb, Eddy Arnold, Hank Williams, Loretta Lynn, Kitty Wells, Jim Reeves, Tex Ritter, Patsy Cline, Jeannie Seely, Mel Tillis, Jan Howard, Grandpa Jones, and many more.

Some of the announcers on the Opry were Grant Turner, Jud Collins, and David Cobb.

When the show hit big over the NBC radio network from Nashville, the host was Whitey Ford who was known as "The Duke of Paducah." The announcer then was Cousin Louie Buck.

The comedic talent on the Opry was filled for a time by two gentlemen by the names of "Lasses and Honey." When Lasses chose to go into other venues, Lee Davis "Honey" Wilds teamed up with Bunny Biggs to form the hilarious "Jam Up and Honey."

Also, on the Opry was a sister act who called themselves, "Sarie and Sally." Their real names were Edna Wilson and Margaret Waters. And, we couldn't leave out Rod Brasfield.

You may remember the colorful country comedian Gilbert R. "Speck" Rhodes. He was that bass playing comic with some teeth blacked out, and garbed in a yellow checkered suit, green derby, and high-buttoned shoes. For a long time, he was associated with Porter Wagoner and the Wagonmasters.

Ralph Emery has done a lot for country music. I am glad that I got to work on six telecasts of *The Ralph Emery Show* on WSM -TV during my short dip into the country music field.

Also, the *Grand Ole Opry* reminds me of RCA Studio B. When you pass by the RCA recording studios on Music Row in Nashville, you will see a building on the corner of Roy Acuff Place and Music Circle, North on which there is a sign which reads, "RCA Studio B." This is probably the most famous studio in the world which for a long time was a tourist attraction. Tourists could go in and see how a real recording studio worked. But, mainly it was a tourist attraction, because this is the studio where many famous artists recorded from Elvis Presley to Elvis Costello.

Some people refer to RCA Studio B as the birthplace of the Nashville Sound. Some other artists holding sessions there were Chet Atkins, Charley Pride, Dolly Parton, Jim Reeves, Roy Orbison, Eddy Arnold, Jerry Reed, Waylon Jennings, the Everly Brothers, and Tammy Wynette.

There were even some non-country artists who recorded there, such as the Monkees, Ann-Margret, Perry Como, and trumpet player Al Hirt.

The studio discontinued its commercial recording there in 1977. Then, the studio was closed to the public in 1998.

In 2002, recording genius, Mike Curb, bought the famed sound studio and leased it back to the Country Music Hall of Fame and Museum for one dollar a year. The studio was restored to its look from the early 1960s, and serves the field of education as a working museum and lab for students of all ages.

I spent a little time in that old Studio B but not as a tourist. I played my first recording date in that studio back in 1971. I was hired to play a session there for a Buck Trent album.

Buck Trent was the banjo and guitar man who worked for many years in Porter Wagoner's band. Buck went on to star on the *Hee Haw* television show.

The recording session was on Monday, November 8, 1971. The album was produced by Bob Ferguson and Porter Wagoner of *Grand Ole Opry* fame both then and now.

In addition to the usual country rhythm section used on

the album, the large orchestra had 4 trumpets, 4 trombones, a flute, 3 B-flat clarinets, and a bass clarinet. I was hired to play the bass clarinet book.

The album by Buck Trent was called *Sounds of Now and Beyond.* I played on two cuts of the album. The two songs are titled, "The Way I See You," and "Until Dawn."

I hope the *Grand Ole Opry* will live forever. By the way, was Goo-Goo candy bar chosen as one of the sponsors because the initials of the *Grand Ole Opry* are GOO?

Of course, when we speak of the Opry, we have to remember the most recognizable of all performers, the Cousin from Grinders Switch, "Minnie Pearl."

I would often see Sarah and Henry Cannon around town. Minnie Pearl was a graduate of the old Ward-Belmont College. Her full name was Sarah Ophelia Colley Cannon.

The real Sarah was nothing even remotely close to the Minnie Pearl character which she portrayed. Sarah was the height of a very shy, dignified, gracious, southern lady. Her name will live forever because of her loving ways, her many generous gifts including the pipe organ at the Brentwood United Methodist Church, and the formation of the Cancer Center in Nashville which bears her name.

Minnie Pearl joined the cast of the *Grand Ole Opry* in December 1940. In 1947, she married Henry Cannon, who became her manager. If you didn't get to see Minnie at the Opry, then you possibly saw her on television when she joined the cast of the long-running syndicated TV show *Hee Haw* in 1969.

Minnie was elected to the Country Music Hall of Fame in 1975. Sadly, her last performance was on June 15, 1991, in Joliet, Illinois. Two days later, she had the first of a series of strokes. Minnie passed away on March 4, 1996. She is buried at Mount Hope Cemetery in Franklin, Tennessee.

"Minnie, we are so proud you were here!"

My friend, retired Elmer Alley, who was a mainstay at WSM radio and television for many years, quoted me the accurate closing spoken by George D. Hay, the Solemn Ole Judge, for each week's performance of the *Grand Ole Opry*. Judge Hay's closing statement each week was:

"That's all for now, friends.
It's time for the tall pines to pine,
the paw paws to pause,
and the bumble bees to bumble all around;
the grasshopper hop, the eaves-droppers drop,
while gently the old cow slips away.
This is George D. Hay saying so long for now."

Then, with two short blasts from his steamboat whistle, the great sounds of the Opry were gone for one week. But, once again the joy and music of our lives blew back in on the next Saturday night for another date with the grandest of all, the *Grand Ole Opry* from Nashville, Tennessee.

Where Did the Big Bands Play in Nashville?

As a young child, I fell in love with the Big Bands. I grew up hearing them, I became a musician and played in them, and now in retirement, I still listen to them.

The Golden Age of the Big Bands really started in the late 1920s and early 1930s after ragtime. Big Bands flourished during the 1940s. Many great songs played by the Big Bands came out of the World War II era. Big Bands even tried to continue on well into the 1950s. Some Big Bands tried to survive even longer, such as Stan Kenton, Woody Herman, Buddy Morrow, Les Brown, and the "ghost" bands of Tommy Dorsey, Glenn Miller, Artie Shaw, and others.

When the Big Bands came into Nashville, where did they play?

One of the famous locations for the Big Bands to perform was at the old Wagon Wheel located where Highways 100 and 70 divide. Many fine bands were booked in there including Tommy Dorsey, Bob Crosby, Glen Gray, Clyde McCoy, Jimmie Lunceford, Cab Calloway, Fats Waller, Jan Garber, Vincent Lopez, Ozzie Nelson, and others.

In the forties, the Plantation Club on Murfreesboro Road had its grand opening. Earl "Fatha" Hines and His Orchestra, featuring Dizzy Gillespie on trumpet and Sarah Vaughan and Billy Eckstine as vocalists, played there for three weeks.

Also, in the late forties, my wife and I heard Jimmy Dorsey and His Orchestra, and Gene Krupa and His Orchestra at the Plantation Club just on one-night-stands.

I got to play the Plantation Club with a band out of Chicago by the name of Henry Brandon and His Orchestra. The band was booked in for two or three weeks, and one of his players had to go back to Chicago, and I got to sub one night playing clarinet and baritone saxophone in the band.

The thing I remember is that Club Plantation featured a professional floor show each night with big acts for which the band played. Later, I remember watching the TV show *Toast of the Town* (The Ed Sullivan Show) and saw one of the acts I played for that night I was there.

The Celtic Room was at the corner of Broadway and 13th Avenue, North. Local bands played there, but sometimes they brought in a Big Name Band. For instance, I was away from Nashville in 1955, but I understand that Louis Armstrong and the All Stars played an exciting performance there on March 3, 1955.

The Hippodrome, which was located on West End Avenue where the Holiday Inn Select Vanderbilt now sits, served as a huge skating rink all week long except for the nights when wrestling was staged, or some other event. Often the Hippodrome would be turned into a convention center or exhibit hall, and sometimes Big Bands would come in and play mostly on one-night-stands.

In the 1940s, I saw Woody Herman and His Orchestra there. I got to hear such great players as Flip Phillips on tenor sax, Red Norvo on vibes, and Bill Harris on trombone. Mary Ann McCall was singing with the band at that time.

Also, in the 1940s, I saw Harry James and His Orchestra at the Hippodrome. Another band I heard there was Elliott Lawrence and His Orchestra. That band drove into town in a fleet of cream colored convertibles.

My friend and Vanderbilt graduate, Ken Berryhill, told

me that Vanderbilt brought in Jimmy Dorsey and His Orchestra to the Hippodrome to play their school dance one year.

The very first band I heard at the Hippodrome was in the late 1930s. I was somewhere around 13 or 14 years old. My sister and I went to the great old Hippodrome skating rink to hear Benny Goodman and His Orchestra playing on a one-night-stand.

If you know anything about the Big Bands, you will appreciate whom we got to see and hear with Goodman's band. Gene Krupa was playing drums, Teddy Wilson was on piano, Lionel Hampton on vibes, and Martha Tilton was his singer.

Ziggy Elman was in the trumpet section. Ziggy Elman had just written "And the Angels Sing." The band played it

PaPa John Gordy's Dixieland Band, Celtic Room c. 1950s
l-r: John Gordy, Young Harper, Dutch Gorton, Harold Bradley,
Clint Garvin, Karl Garvin, and Otto Bash

about six times that night. I am sure they were plugging it since they had just recorded it or planned to record the song.

In addition to these above mentioned places, a Big Band would often come in and play a date at a country club. My friend, Bill Barry of WAMB, told me he remembers when Glen Gray and the Casa Loma Orchestra played a country club here. I remember when Woody Herman played a dinner-dance at the old Maxwell House Hotel.

And, of course, Big Bands would come into Nashville to play at Vanderbilt University, Peabody College, Tennessee State University, and other colleges in the area.

My wife, Sonia, and I were students at Peabody College when Charlie Spivak and His Orchestra played on campus. At Vanderbilt I can remember them bringing into the Old Gym on West End Avenue (which is now the Fine Arts Building minus the old gym) such bands as Buddy Morrow, Tex Beneke, Ralph Flanigan, and others.

One night I saw Lionel Hampton and His Orchestra play a dance at Tennessee State University in their gymnasium.

I remember two jazz clubs on Jefferson Street. One was the Club del Morocco, and the other was the Club Baron. Some artists that played these clubs were Little Richard, Fats Domino, Ray Charles, and Jimi Hendrix.

The Colonial Dinner Club sat near the division of Harding Road and Highway 100. Some nice bands would play there from time to time. Today, at that location you will see the A-1 Appliance Company, but it is not the same building.

The Big Bands were a great part of my life, and certainly a great part of my nostalgic memories. Maybe, you remember too.

Old Radio's Enticing Twosomes

Theme
(Theme fade out behind)
ANNOUNCER: And now, get ready to smile again with radio's homefolk, Vic and Sade, written by Paul Rhymer... Vic and Sade brought to you by the makers of Crisco...

Can any of you remember when we didn't have television in Nashville? Do you remember back to the days when children could be outside playing ball and developing their minds and bodies by socializing and employing teamwork among friends? Children back then didn't stay inside and be glued to a box with a picture on it which might have taught them violence, unacceptable sexual instruction, and bad grammar.

By way of old-time radio announcers, we were exposed to excellent diction, perfect English grammar, and no bad language of any type.

Also, during the old-time radio days, our parents could listen to the radio as they moved around the house doing their chores. Families could listen to radio programs together and not be embarrassed.

My happiness is looking back and listening to the old-time radio days by way of my collection of old radio tapes.

During the Golden Age of Radio (from the mid 1930s through early 1950s) there were many shows comprised of enticing talk between two main characters.

We got to hear about the lives of VIC AND SADE who lived "in the little house halfway up in the next block."

There were LUM AND ABNER, heard daily while they operated Pine Ridge's Jot 'Em Down Store.

There were AMOS AND ANDY, employing their humor among friends at the Fresh Air Taxi Cab Company.

Then, we got to "smile a while" with LORENZO JONES and his devoted wife, BELLE, whose life's struggle had "more smiles than tears."

Who could forget the ABBOTT AND COSTELLO show beginning with Costello's scream, "Hey AA-bbott!"

There were the minstrel humor of PICK AND PAT, the adventures of OZZIE AND HARRIET, the soapy BETTY AND BOB, the spontaneous BOB AND RAY, and the satire of STOOPNAGLE AND BUDD.

There was the comedy-mystery of DETECTIVES BLACK AND BLUE, and the private lives of ETHEL AND ALBERT who lived in "the little town of Sandy Harbor."

FIBBER McGEE AND MOLLY played by real life husband and wife, Jim and Marian Jordan, visited us each week and added pleasure to our lives from their fictitious home at 79 Wistful Vista.

Old radio offered us the scatter-brained humor of the EASY ACES, portrayed by Goodman Ace and his wife, Jane. And, what could have been more scatter-brained than the talk between GEORGE BURNS AND GRACIE ALLEN?

Today during radio "drive time," instead of hearing about sexual harassment, rape, murder, or domestic violence, wouldn't it be nice to hear what two characters had to say about the happiness of life?

Maybe, we would hear Sade tell Vic why she gets Christmas cards in the summer, or the antics of cleaning out an attic, or how Uncle Fletcher is to meet the landlady's fiancee. (All three of those themes were actual program episodes with Vic and Sade.)

I feel certain you would tune in again tomorrow to hear what happiness and wisdom they had to offer.

Nashville's Good Tastes

Whenever I write a column for the *Westview* Newspaper and it includes a variety of memories, I call it a smorgasbord of Nashville's nostalgic tastes. Well, here is a piece that literally identifies some actual Nashville nostalgic tastes—some are gone, and some are with us now.

I am glad that I wrote about Becker's Bakery in my first volume of *Nashville Nostalgia*. I even put a picture of the old bakery in that book. I was surprised when we learned that Becker's Bakery at 12th Avenue, South and Montrose Avenue closed its doors for good on Tuesday, January 6, 2004, after 79 years of operation.

That old bakery went through my childhood, and quite a few of the Becker family members. Frank Becker and his wife, Bethe, owned the bakery for the last seven years. On the day of the closing, it was sad to see the windows covered, and the wide white paper over the front doors. Even that old white paper reminded me of the raisin sweet rolls wrapped in white paper which our Daddy would bring home to us some seventy years ago.

Frank Becker's grandfather, a baker by trade, opened his bakery in 1925 at that 12th Avenue location. On the front door the day that it closed was a sign which read: "After 79 years, we are closing our doors. We have loved being a part of your lives."

My sister, Elva Griffin, and I said that if we had known

they were going to close, we would have stocked up on some of those good old raisin sweet rolls, and maybe a cake or two.

Becker's Bakery on Twelfth Avenue is now part of our memories—part of Nashville Nostalgia; but, we can certainly say, "Thanks, Beckers, for serving us all of those years, and presenting our lives with truly wonderful Nashville nostalgic memories."

———•———

Another tasteful memory which still lives is the Loveless Café on Highway 100 near the entrance to Natchez Trace Parkway. I knew that the McCabes were going to sell the property, but I certainly hoped that the great old tradition could be preserved.

Sure enough, the property was bought by a few committed Nashvillians including Tom Morales, a native Nashvillian who has served the entertainment industry including Hollywood with his TomKats Catering company. My wife, Sonia, and I were served by him once on location when we were involved in a musical production at the Ryman Auditorium.

When the restaurant was bought, Tom said that he would make extensive renovations, but would hold on to the traditions of the great old landmark.

The history of that nationally known restaurant goes back quite a few years. The restaurant opened in 1948 as the Harpeth Valley Tearoom. In 1950, Lon and Annie Loveless bought the restaurant, built a motel on the site, and changed the name of the restaurant to the Loveless Café.

Then, in 1959, Cordell and Stella Maynard bought the restaurant from Mrs. Loveless. In 1973, it was sold to the McCabes. George McCabe and his mother, Donna McCabe, operated the Loveless Café for about 30 years. George is a great-nephew of Charles M. McCabe who once served as the director of our City Parks Administration. Also, he served as Nashville's Postmaster from 1920 until 1923. McCabe Park and Golf Course in West Nashville are named for Charles McCabe.

National magazines have done stories on the Loveless including *Gourmet Magazine*, *Bon Apetit*, *People Magazine*, and *US News and World Report*, as well as the CBS television network. Also, sending mail orders all over the country has made this landmark in Nashville well-known.

Sure enough, the historic Loveless Café, which fronts State Highway 100, reopened on Monday, June 28, 2004, as promised. Ham and fried chicken remain on the menu, but the menu includes some healthier options, too. Loveless will serve vegetables and some non-fried foods.

The dining room is now larger, the kitchen and bath rooms have been renovated, but when you drive up to the entrance, you will see the façade of the structure still reminiscent of the past, even though the outside has been spruced up a bit.

When one enters the restaurant, eyes will gaze upon many photos of celebrities who have eaten there in the past. Willard Scott of the NBC *Today* show stated, "World's greatest scratch biscuits." Martha Stewart made the statement, "It was the best breakfast I've ever had." *People Magazine* called Loveless Country Ham "the best in America."

———————— • ————————

If you are ever in the Krystal on Harding Road close to where Highways 70 and 100 divide, look at a picture on the wall behind the counter. It is a picture of one of the first old Krystal stores in Nashville. I remember them well!

There was an old Krystal on the corner of 21st Avenue, South and Dixie Place across the street from Peabody College where my wife and I used to be customers. The old Krystal stores were rather small, and we sat on stools up at the counter.

Each Krystal store was operated by two men wearing their neat, white uniforms with a black bow tie. They grilled the hamburgers right in front of you.

They would place all of the square-shaped hamburger meat patties on the grill. They would spread some onions across them. After turning them over on the grill, they then placed the buns for each on top of the meat squares while they cooked.

When a customer ordered one, they scooped it up onto a piece of wax paper, served it, and it would literally melt in the mouth of the customer.

We first ate Krystal hamburgers for the price of five cents each. I remember when the price went up to seven cents. Then, I believe they went to a dime, then twelve cents, then maybe fifteen cents, and then on. I really can't remember all of the advancements in price.

I do know what they cost today. They are 57 cents each plus tax. I still like Krystal hamburgers, and I still like my memories of the old days.

———•———

Nashvillians have enjoyed steaks, fish and chicken plus the famous corn cakes at Jimmy Kelly's for more than 60 years. Manager Mike Kelly's grandfather opened the original restaurant in 1935 on Polk Avenue.

Sperry's on Harding Pike is run by Al Thomas, son of Houston Thomas, who opened the restaurant in 1974 with his brother Dick. Sorrowfully, Houston died of cancer in October of 2003. Houston was also involved in other area restaurants including Maude's Courtyard and the Broadway Bakery.

The Elliston Place Soda Shop was named for the Elliston family who owned much of the property in that area. Prior to the present features of the Soda Shop, it was first a grocery store, and then a drugstore.

In 1939, Lynn Chandler, the owner, redesigned half of the structure to form the Soda Shop, and the other half remained a drugstore until 1965. The Elliston Place Soda Shop is ranked as one of the oldest restaurants in Nashville.

For a while, Judge Charles Galbreath owned the soda shop. Today, Eleanor Clay is the owner who also owns the Sylvan Park Restaurant on Murphy Road.

———————•———————

Nashville has enjoyed many wonderful tastes from various restaurants over the years. It is almost sad to mention some that are now just in our memories.

I am thinking of Charlie Nickens Bar-B-Q located on Jefferson Street which had curb service. Edith Trotter, a faithful reader of my weekly column in the *Westview* Newspaper, told me that she has been a menu collector since the early 1950s, and the one she prizes the most is her Charlie Nickens menu in the shape of a pig. Some of you may remember that, too.

I remember the restaurant at the edge of Centennial Park across the street from the old Hippodrome and the present Holiday Inn Select Vanderbilt. I remember when the location was glorified by a great Italian restaurant called Punaro's. It was operated by James Punaro who was a violinist in the Nashville Symphony Orchestra. Many times, the restaurant would be full of guests, and Jimmy Punaro would take out his violin, sit right in the middle of the tables, and begin to play. What a wonderful experience!

After changing hands, the restaurant became the Natchez Trace Restaurant. It served one of the finest and most inexpensive steaks in town. Today, that location is occupied by a McDonald's restaurant and its parking lot.

Do you remember Jack Favier's Silver Wings Restaurant at the old airport? I played in bands for many meetings and conventions at that airport hotel. Then, after the jobs, we would usually eat at the Silver Wings Restaurant.

Do you remember Captain Ray's Sailmaker as a theme restaurant? How many times did you eat at the old Cajun's Wharf on Cowan Street off the Jefferson Street Bridge? Back downtown, I am sure that you picked up some take-out from Zager's Deli on Sixth Avenue.

You will remember "Nashville's Good Tastes" in the cafeterias of our past. Many years ago, Shacklett's Cafeteria was located on Church Street between Fourth and Fifth Avenues, across the street from Burk & Company. Later, the cafeteria moved to the ground floor of the Jackson Building which stood at the corner of Fifth Avenue and Church Street. This was before Cain-Sloan Company moved to that corner from across the street. The cafeteria was founded by Samuel Shacklett who was in the family which settled in the Harpeth Ridge community known as Shacklett just west of Nashville.

You will remember the B & W Cafeteria on Sixth Avenue. When I was in old Boy Scout Troop 26, one of my friends in the troop was Charles Plaxico. His father was the manager of the cafeteria. Charles played accordion, and often you would see him up on the balcony area playing wonderful music for the diners.

Many of us have nostalgia for the old Iris Room in the Cain-Sloan department store. Zanini's had that great, old Italian flavor. And, do you remember eating that wonderful apple pie in Harvey's Downstair's Dinette after Kleeman's closed and Fred Harvey hired the apple pie cook who had worked at Kleeman's?

Many of us used to call that delightful downstair's eating spot at Harvey's "The Luncheonette." After I interviewed Mr. Fred Harvey, Jr. some time back, he informed me that the correct name was Harvey's Downstair's Dinette.

After playing many jobs around town with various orchestras, many of us musicians would meet after the jobs at the old Ireland's across from Vanderbilt, and enjoy those fine steak and biscuits. Out in Green Hills we could eat at Nero's Cactus Canyon. I am sure you have had Melfi's Italian cuisine. Cross Keys was a popular restaurant on Sixth Avenue downtown, as well as the one in the old Green Hills Mall Strip.

Oh, how I miss Marchetti's on Nineteenth Avenue off of West End Avenue. Some mornings I would have coffee there, and talk with many people in the music industry. At noon sometimes I would eat some of that great spaghetti. Then, for some evenings our entire family would go over for delightful meals.

Do you remember the Lazy Susan Restaurant in the Madison Square Shopping Center? The food was served on a large Lazy Susan in the middle of the table which you would turn to get a second helping of whatever you liked. A son of Dr. and Mrs. Fred Overton owned and operated that fun restaurant.

My wife, Sonia, and I went to Varallo's on Church Street on December 30, 1998, to order our last bowl of chili-three-ways. That is the day that Varallo's closed their Church Street doors for good. We waited in a long line that day to get in which was fine. I remember that we sat near the table of John J. Hooker and many other notable Nashvillians.

After talking about all of those good Nashville tastes, I wish we could go and enter other nostalgic locations to top off the meal with a good dessert. Would you rather have a Black Walnut Angel Whip at the Frozen Castle on Gallatin Road, or a Marshmallow Nut Sundae with those little chocolate spriggles on top at Candyland?

Did You Know Bettie Page?

Our son, Jeff Thompson, teaches English and Writing Skills at Tennessee State University. He is also a specialist in Pop Culture. Several times he has asked me, "Did you know Bettie Page at George Peabody College?" At Peabody, Bettie was an English major, and worked as a secretary to Dr. Alfred Leland Crabb. But, I had to answer, "I really can't place her, and don't think that I knew her."

In case you are not familiar with the name Bettie Page, I should tell you that she was a model, and has appeared in more magazines than Marilyn Monroe and Cindy Crawford combined. Bettie worked as a model for only seven years (1950-1957). She married, became very religious, attended Bible college, and is now retired and lives in California according to her brother who still lives in Nashville.

Bettie, living in seclusion, isn't even aware that she is still listed as a pop culture icon. Remaining relatively unknown, she is known today as "Queen of the Pin-ups."

Even the 1982 comic book, *The Rocketeer*, modeled the female lead after Bettie. The name "Betty" was even given to this female lead. The comic became a major motion picture by Walt Disney Studios in 1991. The real Bettie Page is currently featured on more than 100,000 websites.

A reporter found her in California, and Bettie was stunned to learn of her ever-growing popularity. She said that she finds all the fuss mystifying. At age 80, Bettie grants few interviews and refuses to be photographed.

I thought no more about my son asking me if I knew Bettie Page until I read a feature story written by Mary Tom Bass about Bettie in the Winter 2003 issue of the *Peabody Reflector*, a Vanderbilt University publication which is mailed to the Peabody College alumni.

Bettie graduated from Hume-Fogg High School. I attended Hume-Fogg High School for the 1939-1940 school year. Bettie was a sponsor of the R. O. T. C. at Hume-Fogg. I was in the R. O. T. C. for the year I attended.

After graduating from high school, Bettie went to George Peabody College where she majored in English. To help meet tuition expenses, Bettie worked as a secretary to the late Dr. Alfred Leland Crabb, highly respected professor and author. I studied with Dr. Crabb at Peabody.

Bettie typed manuscripts for at least three of Dr. Crabb's eleven historical novels and books. She typed the manuscripts from Dr. Crabb's handwritten notes and dictation. When I was in Dr. Crabb's office in the old Administration Building at Peabody, I wonder if I saw and spoke to Miss Bettie Page?

As I read this story in the *Peabody Reflector*, I was amazed that I did not know Bettie at Peabody College. It seems that I was always a little ahead or behind her in many groups and activities.

Bettie was interested in drama, and joined the Peabody Players who did play productions. I was in the Peabody Players. In fact, that is where I met Sonia Anne Young, who would later become my wife.

Bettie was a member of the Peabody Players Radio Guild which broadcast 15 minutes each Saturday morning over radio station WLAC. I played as a musician at WLAC in 1941.

Two people that were interviewed for this story in the *Peabody Reflector* were Barbara Gatwood and James Maddux. I was a classmate of Barbara. Her father was once the Head of the Music Department at Peabody College. Also, Sonia and I both as Peabody Players were in a play titled *Death Takes a Holiday* which starred our friend Jimmy Maddux. Both of these two students who were interviewed for the magazine article knew Bettie, and both said that Bettie was extremely shy and kept pretty much to herself.

Bettie received her B.A. degree in English in 1944. I was a student at Peabody part of 1942 and 1943 before I went into the Army during World War II.

Bettie returned to Peabody College in the mid-1960s to work on a graduate degree. Well, I took a leave-of-absence from my teaching job at Evansville College in Indiana for the 1963-64 school year to attend Peabody to work on a graduate degree.

So, after reading that story about Bettie Page in the *Peabody Reflector*, I have to say that maybe I did know Bettie Page at Peabody College after all. Maybe I do remember her. Maybe my wife knew her, too. Yes, I now think I will have to answer, "Yes, I knew Bettie Page."

A Living Legend

The year was 1979. It was an emotional time for the legion of past Peabody College music majors. The Peabody Board of Trustees voted to dissolve the music department at George Peabody College for Teachers. The teacher's college was to merge with Vanderbilt University becoming the College of Education at Vanderbilt and renamed "George Peabody College of Vanderbilt University." And, Blair School of Music would become the music school of Vanderbilt.

Time marches on, but nothing can erase the memories of an institution which contributed so much to the musical culture of a city—even the world.

Thousands of artist-teachers passed through the beautiful pillars of the Social-Religious Building as music students. In fact, some of my greatest memories are the times we sat in the rocking chairs on the gigantic front porch of the building and learned from some who would later become the top music teachers, conductors, singers, instrumentalists, composers, arrangers, and stars in the world of music.

Today, I often refer to the particular professors who taught me certain skills which I carried on through my life in music. They were giants in their field.

In June of 1979, Sonia and I realized what was to come with regard to the up-coming merger of Peabody and Vanderbilt. We wrote a note to Professor Louis Nicholas who was one of those beloved music professors at Peabody, and was the remaining professor who had the longest years of service in the Peabody music department.

Sonia and I could feel a little of what the emotions of Louis Nicholas must have been on that final day of the Peabody College music department in 1979.

Of course, there are many advantages for Peabody being the College of Education at Vanderbilt University. But, some memories are impossible to repeat.

It has been a long time since I was seventeen years old and enrolled as a freshman music major at Peabody College. It has been a long time since I met Sonia Anne Young in that English department Play Production class and whom would later become my wife.

Today, both Sonia and I are retired. Well, not really. Music is still in our lives through many activities.

In cleaning out some of my files, (being born just before The Great Depression, I never seem to throw away anything) I ran across the letter of response which Louis Nicholas sent to Sonia and me after we had lovingly written to him so many years ago.

This is the letter that Louis Nicholas wrote to us on the very last day of classes before the music department at Peabody was closed. The letter is dated June 29, 1979. I am certain I could not read the letter out loud without becoming emotional. However, I want to place it in print for you to read:

Dear E. D. and Sonia,

Thank you for your assurance of support. Today, the last day of classes before Vanderbilt takes over, I thought of the poignance of a short story of Alphonse Daudet which I read many years ago. It is called 'La Derniere Classe' and it tells of the takeover by the Germans of Alsace after the defeat of France in the War of

1870.

Long after, a grown man recalls 'The Last Class' held in the little school he attended before German became the official language. Many of the older townspeople came and sat under the old schoolmaster that day. He had been there forty years, and had taught most of them.

Young and old went through their lessons industriously as if it were the last day—as indeed it was. At its close, overcome by emotion and unable to speak, the old schoolmaster turned to the blackboard and wrote with all his might 'Vive la France! Long live France!'

That is quite how I felt today. Keep a warm spot in your hearts for the Peabody that was, as I shall always do.

Sincerely,
Louis Nicholas

Louis Nicholas continued to live in Nashville for many years after the closing of Peabody's music department. We would see him at the Symphony concerts and other musical presentations around the city.

Not long ago, Professor Nicholas, who is in his nineties, moved to Memphis where he is closer to some family members. We miss seeing him in Nashville, but we wish him good health, happiness, and the very best of everything.

"We shall never forget you Professor Louis Nicholas, a Living Legend!"

Nashville Hotels of Our Nostalgic Past

If I were asked, "What is the greatest and most tragic loss in Nashville's past?" it would not take any thought at all for me to quickly answer, "The Maxwell House Hotel."

The history surrounding the hotel alone is something that can make your head reel. John Overton, Jr. began building the hotel prior to the Civil War. Work was stopped during the war. In fact, the portion of the hotel which had been built was used by the Union troops as a barracks, prison, and hospital after Nashville was captured.

Following the war, Overton Jr., known as "The Colonel," owned his father's financial empire and finished the hotel. The grand hotel was opened in 1869.

When I played many jobs with bands at the Maxwell House, I was always in awe as I walked into the lobby where I was surrounded by the elegance of the great atrium with its marble columns. I was awe-inspired as I walked up the grand open staircase, as I moved onto the plush mezzanine, and into the grand ballroom, realizing that I was walking in the footsteps of many famous people, including generals and presidents of this nation.

Read Alfred Leland Crabb's historical novel titled *Supper at the Maxwell House*, and you will read of dinners and dances held in that giant, historic edifice at the corner of old Cherry Street (Fourth Avenue, North) and Church Street back at the close of the Civil War. In the 1940s, (some 75 years after the Civil War) I played many dinner-dances in that same ballroom.

There have been so many hotels with such wonderful memories in Nashville's past.

The Andrew Jackson Hotel stood for many years at the corner of Sixth Avenue, North and Deaderick Street where our present James K. Polk State Office Building and the Tennessee Performing Arts Center stand today.

When Francis Craig and His Orchestra was playing and broadcasting from the Grill Room of the Hermitage Hotel, other bands were being broadcast on remotes from the Andrew Jackson Hotel. Also, this hotel was the chosen meeting place back in the days of the old Dee Jay Conventions.

The Tulane Hotel at the corner of Eighth Avenue, North and Church Street has to be in the history books for being the location of Nashville's first recording company. Around 1945,

Maxwell House Hotel, c. 1925

three radio engineers who were with WSM radio—Aaron Shelton, George Reynolds, and Carl Jenkins—opened Castle Studio in the old Tulane Hotel.

The Noel Hotel building is still sitting at the corner of Fourth Avenue, North and Church Street. It is now the offices of Prudential Securities. Only our past memories can see in our minds the old lobby, the ballroom, the morning breakfast club program of WLAC radio which I can recall, and the dining room. The Noel Hotel dining room was one of the best in town.

The Sam Davis Hotel was a fixture downtown for many years until it was razed in 1984. The James Robertson Hotel still stands on Seventh Avenue downtown, but it is no longer a hotel. It has been converted to apartment living.

The Duncan Hotel was located at the corner of Fourth Avenue and Cedar Street (Charlotte Avenue.) That hotel was a little before my time, but I include it because I have seen pictures of that hotel, and it was very distinguished looking.

The Allen Hotel was located at 2004 West End Avenue. It was noted for having a very fine restaurant. I remember delivering some lead sheets which I had written for an out-of-town songwriter who was staying at the Allen Hotel. (I wonder why I didn't have him pick them up at my office table beside the pay phone at Tex Ritter's Restaurant where I started my music company?)

In the old days, do you remember when salesmen were called "drummers?" Many of them used to stay at the old Savoy Hotel.

The Anchor was considered to be Nashville's first downtown motel. It was located at 20th Avenue and West End. Today, a Hampton Inn is located there.

Of course, Nashville has seen many other hotels come and go, such as The Clarkston, Argonne, Underwood, Merchants, Utopia, and Bismarck.

Nashville is blessed by still having many fine hotels. Downtown alone we have the Union Station Hotel, Courtyard by Marriott, Doubletree Hotel, Hilton Suites Nashville Downtown, Renaissance Nashville Hotel, Sheraton Nashville Downtown, Loew's Vanderbilt Plaza Hotel, The Hermitage Hotel, and others.

The Hermitage Hotel, which opened in 1910 and is now listed on the national register of historical places, went under extensive renovation, and stands today among the fine, elegant hotels of the past.

Fifty years from now, maybe someone will write about some of these great hotels in bringing some nostalgic happiness to some other readers.

Hillsboro High's Harrowing Halloween

It was October 31, 1952. Halloween! I was living on Warfield Drive in Green Hills.

Warfield Drive was only several blocks from Hillsboro High School where I taught from 1948 after I graduated from George Peabody College until 1954 when I got married.

On this particular October morning of 1952, my telephone rang about 6:30 A. M. I answered the phone to hear the frantic voice of Mrs. Thackston, a history teacher at the high school, shouting, "Thompson, Hillsboro High is burning down!"

I, quite miffed, retorted, "Mrs. Thackston, it is 6:30 in the morning. It is too early in the morning to be playing Halloween jokes."

Mrs. Thackston responded, "No, I am serious. Hillsboro is burning to the ground."

I hung up the telephone, and ran to my upstairs window, and sure enough, I could see black, billowing smoke rising into the sky over in the Hillsboro High area.

I quickly threw on my clothes, got in my car, and headed over to the high school.

I had to park a short distance from the school due to the traffic, police, and fire engines. I dashed up to the front of the burning building. Mr. John Koen, the school principal, ran up to me, threw his arms around me, and said, "Thompson, it's gone, it's gone!"

I immediately saw three of my band students. One said that he had recovered two of the band instruments. Then, these three students and I ran to the rear of the building where the band room was located. We were able to go in and pull out some more instruments including some of the drums which were set up on drum stands.

Before we could continue working, a policeman came and ordered us out as the firemen were beginning to move into that area of the building.

For the remainder of the morning, we had to sit and watch the building burn to the ground. My understanding was that the fire was caused by an electrical problem located in the area of the cafeteria.

A number of election voting machines for that community of the county had been temporarily stored in Hillsboro High's gymnasium. The machines also were burned up in the fire. It created a

The school burned in 1952

problem for the upcoming election, but nothing was found to be connected to the machines and the fire. It was just an inconvenience for the voters to go to another location.

More and more of the high school band students began to assemble. We had to make some plans. The school had a football game that night, and the band had a half-time show to do.

Some of the students contacted the local television and radio stations to ask them to make an announcement.

The stations were happy to announce that the band director had called a special band rehearsal that day at two o'clock, and that the football game with Montgomery Bell Academy was still on as scheduled.

Most of the band students had their musical instruments safely at home. Fortunately, every band student had his and her uniform safely at home.

I quickly made calls to other band directors for help. I learned that West End High School had played their football game the night before.

Thanks to Mr. D. F. Bain, my friend and the band director at West End High, we were able to borrow some of their drums, a sousaphone, and a few other instruments.

At two o'clock sharp, the entire

Looking at the ruins

Hillsboro High School Band assembled on the football field behind the burning building. The drum major, Ogden Stokes, blew his whistle to begin the final drill for our half-time show for the night's football game.

Tears filled everyone's eyes as we held a regular band class. The difference this day was that we were playing show tunes and marches while we watched our beloved building smolder, and watched the walls collapse from the fire.

The football game was held that night on the Montgomery Bell Academy field. The Hillsboro football team had borrowed uniforms from Father Ryan High School since their game also was played the night before.

M. B. A. was favored to win the game that night, but I can recall, Hillsboro won the ball game. The final score was Hillsboro 19, and Montgomery Bell Academy 0.

The band's half-time show came off quite well. Before the band left the field, I conducted the school's "Alma Mater."

In that cold, damp, Fall night, there was hush silence from the spectators on both sides of the field. You could see the tears in the eyes of everyone of us as we played and listened to our "Alma Mater."

Principal John Koen went to work to keep the school's student body together. He was determined, and was successful in his efforts. For the remainder of that year and the next year, Hillsboro High students met classes in rooms at Belmont Methodist Church and Belmont College.

From the "Alma Mater" to our memories of more than a half of a century ago, we can say, "Viva la Hillsboro High School by way of the many strong students of outstanding character who graduated from that Davidson County institution of learning, its many fine teachers, and its very effective and compassionate principal, Mr. John Koen."

Wallace Edwards
& E.D.T.

At one class session of the classes I taught on "Nashville Nostalgia" for the Retirement Learning at Vanderbilt program during the Winter of 2001, we talked about Hillsboro High School burning in 1952. I found out that four people in the class were at Hillsboro as students. One of them, Wallace Edwards, played first clarinet in the band which I directed. I had not seen Wallace for almost fifty years.

During that class, I made the statement that I owned all of the Hillsboro

High annuals during the years I taught there except one. I mentioned that the one I did not have was the 1952-53 annual which covered the fire.

The next class session, Wallace brought me a copy of that annual as a gift. What a treasure!

There are always a lot of stories to come from such a happening as this tragic fire. Let me tell you one about *The Canterbury Tales* by Chaucer.

Prior to this devastating fire at our school, an English teacher had assigned this Middle English Narrative Poetry to a class. As you know, some of it is rather risqué. A student's father had read it, went to the principal, and demanded that it not be assigned to his daughter's class.

In the old days, we didn't make a federal case out of everything. If possible, we just solved problems. So, Principal John Koen felt that if the assignment was offensive, then he would just have the book sent to the office. He felt that there was certainly enough other literature to be assigned.

It was such a horror to realize that our building burned down on that fatal day, and even our wonderful library with all of the thousands of books were burned up. That is, all but one.

The copy of Chaucer's *The Canterbury Tales* had been placed in the metal vault in the office, so it did not burn!

From Antebellum, to Colemere, to Catfish

An old antebellum home was originally built on Murfreesboro Road, near our present airport, in the late 1800s, and served as the country estate of Colonel Edmund W. Cole who was an important railroad executive in Nashville.

The mansion was built on 17 acres of grounds. There was a grand, limestone and iron gate leading up the driveway to a porte cochere where carriages could park under a roof to protect the passengers. The mansion had two half-oval side porches which were quite distinctive features of the home.

A damaging fire struck the mansion back in 1929. But, in 1931 Cole's youngest daughter and her husband, Dempsey Weaver, designed another home in the style of a Natchez, Mississippi antebellum mansion.

In 1940, this home was acquired by the City of Nashville. We saw the elite of our city including the city's political set develop a country club there which was used from 1948 until 1973 when the country club closed.

We knew it as the Colemere Country Club. I played many dinner-dances there for the elite of our great city.

In 1977, the mansion was altered and shaped to become what we see there today as the New Orleans Seafood Manor on Murfreesboro Road next to the Airport.

But, between the times of Cole's country home, and the present seafood restaurant, that old antebellum home location was a stylish country club where the elite would meet, greet and eat. Nashville's Big Bands played there every Saturday night plus on other special occasions.

The Colemere Country Club was organized on January 9, 1948. I played in the band near the time of the opening of the Colemere Club in 1948. At that time, I was playing with Tommy Knowles and His Orchestra.

Then, my own band, Buddy Thompson and The Nashville Knights, played the last dinner-dance at the Colemere before it closed in 1973. I always wanted my own dance orchestra. I had a dance band in high school, I had a band in college during the 1940s, and then I booked my band, "The Nashville Knights," from the years 1971 until 1985. The Colemere Country Club closed following the New Year's Eve dinner-dance which we played on Monday night, December 31, 1973.

I wish I could count the number of Saturday nights that I played at the Colemere Country Club with other bands. My wife, Sonia, often accompanied me to those events. The Colemere Club members were the elite leaders of our city. It was a pleasure for us to meet many of them.

Often on Saturday nights, the members would bring out celebrities, who happened to be in town, as their guests. If any of them were singers, the band would accompany them.

I can remember when the Dinning Sisters came out on one Saturday night and sang several numbers. The band read the arrangements they brought with them. The Dinning Sisters used to appear on the old WLS Barn Dance in Chicago as well as other national programs.

Once Jimmy Wakely and Margaret Whiting came out as someone's guests. The band got to play their accompaniment for their big, hit song at the time called "Slippin' Around."

When I was in the Army during World War II, I spent almost all of my free time going to movies. I very much admired a movie star by the name of Joan Leslie who appeared in many of the movies of that era.

One Saturday night, not too long after the war, I was playing in the band at the Colemere Club. I just about fell out of my chair when one of the club members entered the door escorting his guest who was none other than Joan Leslie. She was in Nashville for some kind of a promotion, and was invited to the Colemere Club. Believe me, I would have worked that night for free!

———•———

Following a column I wrote in the *Westview* Newspaper about the Colemere Club, my friend and neighbor in Bellevue, Everett Templeton, called me and said that he had an old membership list around the time I was playing there in the 1960s. Temp said that he received it from his father-in-law who was one of the Colemere members at the time. I think you should enjoy seeing some of the Nashvillians who were members of the old Colemere Country Club. Their names should bring back a lot of memories to you old Nashvillians, and even younger citizens will recognize many names.

Just to mention a few politicians, some members were Governor Buford Ellington, Governor Frank Clement (who was an attorney at the time), Senator Albert Gore Senior, Senator Estes Kefauver, Congressman J. Carlton Loser, and Mayor Ben West.

William B. Akers with Asphalt Products Company was a member. He did a lot of good work in the Boy Scouts. A. G. Alessio with the Automobile Club was a member.

Some of you will remember Robert J. Anderson of Anderson Fish & Oyster Company. I remember realtor Glenn

Bainbridge, and Bob Battle who was a great writer for the *Nashville Banner.*

By the way, mentioning all of these names also means that their wives were always with them, too.

There was Alvin G. Beaman of the Seven-Up Bottling Co. Florist Harold Bennett was a member. I went to school with some of the Bennetts. Houston Blazer of Blazer Brothers was a member, and he was a saxophone player, too.

Many of us knew James V. Blevins who owned Blevins Popcorn Company. Jim was a happy fellow, and made everyone around him feel good.

Owen Bradley, the big name in music and recording, was a member. There was Clydell Castleman with the Nashville Mid-Tennessee Auto Club. Another member was Edwin W. Craig of National Life & Accident Insurance Co. He was a relative of band leader Francis Craig. Another member was Wilbur F. Creighton, Jr. of Foster & Creighton.

You remember Sam M. Fleming of the Third National Bank. There was attorney Elkin Garfinkle, Richard D. Gleaves, who was a state official and attorney, Fred O. Gossett of M. T. Gossett Company, and real estate man Henry A. Gupton.

I knew Herschel Greer and his lovely wife. Herschel was with Guaranty Mortgage Company, and his family and my family were members of the same church. Also, around the year 1962, Herschel was the vice-president of the Colemere Country Club.

Nashville lawyer John J. Hooker was a member. I remember Edward F. Jones of the Nashville Flying Service. Luke Lea who began *The Nashville Tennessean* was a member. Another member was Dr. John J. Lentz who was the Davidson County Health Director.

Other members were Harry Lipman of Lipman

Brothers, Aubrey A. Maxwell of A. O. Maxwell Co., and Johnny Mihalic who used to be the second baseman for the old Nashville Vols baseball team. In the 1960s, Johnny had moved on to become a big executive at AVCO Corporation.

I remember contractor Allan Murphy and his wife. I taught their son, Dick Murphy, at Hillsboro High School back in the early 1950s. One of the finest newspaper columnists was a member. His name was Red O'Donnell who wrote a popular column in the Nashville daily newspapers at different times.

There was James H. Reed, Jr. of Jim Reed Chevrolet, photographer Henry Schofield, and a retired surgeon, Dr. H. H. Shoulders.

Lawyer Cecil Sims was a member. He was on the Davidson County school board when I taught at Hillsboro High School. Another Colemere member was John Sloan of Cain-Sloan Company.

You may remember radio man Jack Stapp. Jack was the talent man at WSM radio. He hired Fannie Rose Shore (Dinah Shore), and many other singers and actors. Later, Jack organized Tree International, which became the largest country music publisher in our music industry.

You will remember Nick F. Varello who at the time had Nick Varello's Drive-In. Another member was Morris Zager who owned Morris Zager's Restaurant.

You remember the Werthan Bag Company, and the contribution they made to our city and to America. These four Werthans were honorary members: Albert, Bernard, Howard, and Joe Werthan.

The Colemere Club was a wonderful place for musicians to play. The people were great. During the summer months, the bands played on an outdoor bandstand overlooking the airport. We could see the planes coming in and taking off while we sat there on the bandstand.

Sadly, many of these fine old Nashvillians have passed away. And, the last time I drove by the old Colemere home on Murfreesboro Road, I noticed that the outside bandstand where the orchestras used to play on the terrace in the summertime had been removed.

I remember one summer dinner-dance in 1963 when I played with the Bob Hamp Orchestra out on the outdoor terrace bandstand. Bob was my brother-in-law, and had a fine band. Radio station WFMB-FM (105.9 on the FM dial), which was owned at the time by Bill Baird and Bill Barry, who is now the owner of radio station WAMB (the Big Band station), came out and did an hour-long remote broadcast of the band on their radio station.

I hope the names of these outstanding Nashvillians and businesses will bring back some nice nostalgic memories to your mind. I have named just a few members, but you can see that the Colemere Country Club was made up of the elite of this city which made Nashville grow and become a city in which we can be very proud.

The Songbird of the South

Two of my many loves are Old Time Radio, and the Big Band Era. Let me put these two together, and tell you about the wonderful singer, Kate Smith.

I will not start with when I worked with her. That will come later. Let me start as a child when I loved to listen to our old Majestic radio in our living room and hear *The Kate Smith Hour.*

Kate was first heard on network radio by way of NBC back in 1931. Later, in the mid-thirties over CBS, Kate starred as *The Songbird of the South* with Jack Miller's Orchestra, and was sponsored by the Hudson Motor Car Company. I recall that one of her guests on a program was Dizzy Dean, the baseball pitcher. (Baseball is another one of my loves.)

Kate Smith on radio continued into the 1940s and 50s. I remember some of her other radio sponsors were the Great Atlantic and Pacific Tea Company, Calumet Baking Soda, Swans Down Flour, Grapenuts, Jello, and Postum, among others.

I especially enjoyed hearing Kate Smith on radio when her announcer and co-host was Ted Collins. Ted was also Kate's manager for many years.

A great milestone in music occurred on November 11, 1938 on Armistice Day (which we now call Veterans Day) when Kate Smith introduced Irving Berlin's "God Bless America" which Kate sang on into musical immortality.

Irving Berlin's "God Bless America" lifted America from the deep valley of despair following 911. The song used to be reserved for the Fourth of July celebrations. But, in reality, the great song is used in America almost daily throughout the entire year.

In August of 1918, Irving Berlin, who served in the U. S. Army during World War I, was granted special leave to produce a soldier show called *Yip, Yip, Yaphank*. The composer wrote all of the songs in the show, including the old favorite which you might remember, "Oh, How I Hate to Get Up in the Morning."

As the story is told, Irving Berlin composed "God Bless America" during a rehearsal of that show, but he found that the song just didn't fit with the other things in the snappy, fast-moving show.

Berlin had a trunk in his home where he stored songs which didn't fit at the moment, or he felt that he couldn't market. So, "God Bless America" found its dark grave in that trunk, and remained locked in that trunk in his attic for twenty years.

In 1938, Kate Smith was America's queen of the airwaves, and "The first lady of radio." Ted Collins, her show's producer, received a call from Washington, D. C. The United States was at peace, but Hitler's Germany was rattling its weapons in Europe. Our leaders in Washington wanted Kate to introduce a new, patriotic song that Americans could adopt.

Ted Collins called Irving Berlin to ask for his help. As the story goes, Berlin spent endless hours trying to come up with a suitable, patriotic song, but nothing seemed right to him. Even with geniuses, words and music may not blend perfectly all the time.

Ted Collins announced on Kate's show that her next broadcast would feature a new patriotic song by the great Irving Berlin. Berlin had only one week before Kate's radio broadcast. Then, Berlin remembered his trunk in the attic. He pulled out

"God Bless America" which was originally written for *Yip, Yip, Yaphank* during World War I.

Berlin had a messenger carry a copy of the song to the CBS radio studios where the Kate Smith show was already in rehearsal. The singer loved the new song. It was first performed by her on that radio show in 1938, and it has been in our lives ever since.

———•———

Around the early 1970s, Kate Smith came to Nashville for a concert while on tour. The only four people who came with her were Mitchell Ayres, who was the orchestra leader; Archie Bleyer, who was the musical arranger; Moe Wetsel, a fine piano man from New York; and Kate's make-up and hair stylist. The large orchestra was hired in Nashville.

You may remember Mitch Ayres who was the orchestra leader for the *Perry Como Shows* on television, and the *Hollywood Palace* television shows.

You may remember the name, Archie Bleyer, from the old Arthur Godfrey radio shows. He was the band leader.

In Nashville they hired a big orchestra of 5 saxophones, 4 trumpets, 4 trombones, a French Horn, a rhythm section, and about 8 or 10 strings. I was hired to play the book which called for baritone saxophone and bass clarinet. That was one of the finest bands with which I ever had the pleasure of working.

Nashville's Big Band leader Red McEwen booked the band in Nashville. He used to book many acts when they came into Nashville. I got to play a lot of shows with him including the Shrine Circus, the Ringling Brothers Barnum & Bailey Circus, Holiday on Ice, concerts by Englebert Humperdink, Sonny and Cher, and others.

Kate Smith was a wonderful singer. She was just as great in being a gentle, gracious, lovely, southern lady.

After we played her concert in Nashville, the next day we got on the band bus and headed for Knoxville where we did the same concert at Knoxville's Convention Center.

When Kate ended the programs with "God Bless America," there was a spirit and feeling that came over the entire audience that seemed to make everyone proud to be an American.

My son, Jeff Thompson, an announcer at WAMB Big Band radio in Nashville, plays some good Kate Smith music on various patriotic days.

If you want to get the musical thrill of your life, tune in and hear Kate Smith when she sings "God Bless America" on her live performance taped at Carnegie Hall in New York City. The audience is spellbound. At the last note, the audience gives Kate a standing ovation, and the only way she can silence them is to go into her theme song, "When the Moon Comes Over the Mountain." It was the same when I played her concerts in Nashville and Knoxville.

Kate Smith is a musical legend. She rightfully deserves the two titles of "The first lady of radio," and "The Songbird of the South."

Old Television Revisited

When television first came to Nashville in 1950 by way of WSM-TV, channel 4, how many of you sat and stared at the black-and-white TV test pattern until the first program came on? That television station today is WSMV, channel 4.

Jack DeWitt was a world-class broadcast engineer. He was a colonel in the Army Signal Corps during World War II. He was able to bounce radar off of the moon. Jack had such recognition and respect that he was able to get the first television station licensed and on the air in Nashville.

Back in those days, network signals traveled on coaxial cables, and the co-ax only came as far as Louisville coming south out of Chicago. Jack DeWitt built and wholly owned a microwave link from Nashville to Louisville, so he could get the programs and network television in Nashville first.

If we think back on old television programs of the 1950s and 1960s, it is not hard to remember such network shows as *Father Knows Best, I Love Lucy, My Three Sons*, Milton Berle's *Texaco Star Theatre, Playhouse 90, The Red Skelton Show, The Ed Sullivan Show, The Show of Shows* with Imogene Coca and Sid Caesar, and many more.

Even my wife, Sonia, and I appeared on national TV back in 1954. We were married on the NBC television program *Bride and Groom*. It originated from the Hudson Theatre in New York City, the same theatre which at night televised the Steve Allen show, which eventually became the *Tonight Show*.

After our week's honeymoon at Goshen Inn in Goshen,

New York, which was just one of the many gifts we received for appearing on the program, we returned to Manhattan. Early one morning, we walked down to Rockefeller Center and stood at the window looking at the *Today* show, which then starred Dave Garroway. When we arrived back in Nashville the next day, my mother told us that she had seen us looking in the window at the NBC *Today* show.

By the way, one of the guests on the show that day was James Melton, who had attended Vanderbilt and had sung for about three years with the Francis Craig Orchestra at the Grill Room of the Hermitage Hotel in Nashville. Both Melton and Dave Garroway came out on the sidewalk beside us during one segment of the morning show for Jimmy Melton to show Dave some of his antique car collection.

National television was one thing, but do you ever think back about those old TV shows that were produced locally? How about *Ruff and Ready,* seen on channel 4? The actor using that name presented great western movies for the kids each afternoon along with his interesting talk and humor.

When television was still young in Nashville, I remember going out to the WSIX-TV (then channel 8) studio. It was a concrete building right under their tall TV tower off of Old Hickory Boulevard near Brentwood which they referred to as "The Hill." I walked in and saw a favorite Nashville disc jockey by the name of Noel Ball, who had a live TV show called *Saturday Showcase.*

In 1961, WSIX-TV and the WSIX-AM and FM radio stations moved to some nice acreage of prime industrial land on Murfreesboro Road where WKRN-TV operates today. By the way, Archie Boone, who was Pat Boone's father, was the contractor who built the facility.

Then, many of you remember that on December 11,

1973, WSIX, channel 8, exchanged channels with our public television station WDCN, channel 2. When this exchange was made, WSIX-TV began operating as WNGE-TV, channel 2, which it still is today, but called WKRN-TV 2.

You probably remember Hudley Crockett, who I believe was the first news man on camera at WSIX-TV. You probably

Ken Bramming

remember Tom Siler, who was known as the "Weather Wizard".

On channel 4 you might remember Dave Overton, who had a show called *Five O'Clock Hop*.

Shock and horror films were a big attraction. The great radio voice of Ken Bramming was heard on WSIX-TV, channel 8 television. Ken was seen made up as Dr. Lucifur as he introduced horror movies to his audience. He entertained

through a program called *Shock Theatre* from 1958 until 1967 on WSIX-TV, as well as a Friday night chiller called *Mystic Circle* on the old TV channel 17, with such movie characters as Frankenstein and Dracula.

Before Ken Bramming passed away in 1997, he was an announcer and program director at Nashville's nostalgic WAMB Big Band radio station. Our son, Jeff Thompson, worked with Ken Bramming at radio station WAMB until Ken's death. Jeff has some of Ken's memorabilia, which includes the only tape footage in existence of Dr. Lucifur doing his *Shock Theatre* show.

In 2003, Channel 2 used the footage on its fiftieth-anniversary show.

In 1990, while my wife Sonia, Jeff, and I were in Los Angeles, we went out to the Hollywood Hills to the home of Forrest J. Ackerman, who is called "Mr. Science Fiction" and the patriarch of fantasy fandom.

Ken Bramming as Dr. Lucifur

His home used to be the home of Jon Hall, who you might remember played *Ramar of the Jungle* many years ago. Forry (as fans call him) had a house full of movie memorabilia. It was a thrill to see Bela Lugosi's Dracula cape, Lon Chaney's makeup kit, and Ray Harryhausen's miniature dinosaurs.

While we were in Forry's home, who should walk in the door but Julius Schwartz, who was the editor of *Superman* and *Flash* comic books for more than fifty years. I took a photograph of Jeff standing between Forry Ackerman and Julie Schwartz.

Recently, two independent filmmakers interviewed Jeff at his home for a documentary they are filming about local TV horror movie hosts from around the country to be titled *American Scary*. They were interested in much of what Jeff had to offer with regard to this pop culture.

As Jeff stated on the interview, "Many horror films being made today are too bloody and dirty for children and young people to see. Back in the old days, the films were fun, interesting, and a delight for all members of the family to enjoy."

Russ McCown was a former film director at old WSM-TV, channel 4. Russ retired from WSMV-TV back in 1988 after a 35-year career. Back in the 1960s, Russ developed a character called Sir Cecil Creape; and, in addition to performing short skits, he introduced horror films on a show called *Creature Feature*.

Then, around 1970, my friend, Elmer Alley, who was the program director at channel 4 at the time, told Russ it would be nice if he could bring Sir Cecil out again. At that particular time, horror films were making another big sweep over the country.

So, Sir Cecil Creape and his *Creature Feature* aired at 10:30 PM on Saturday nights on channel 4 from 1971 until about 1973. I understand that Elmer Alley started out writing the scripts, but I read from an interview by Ken Beck that channel four's former weatherman, Pat Sajak of *Wheel of Fortune* fame, wrote several of the scripts, also.

Around 1983, when Elmer Alley was looking around for some programs to go on the newly formed Nashville Network, Sir Cecil Creape came out again. He moved his crypt from the WSMV studios to the catacombs underneath the Grand Ole Opry House for his *Phantom of the Opry* horror film series, and stayed for several years on the TNN cable network.

On old WSIX television we got to see Jim Kent, who was featured as Captain Crook on a children's show. Jim's two sons also were active on that show. Jim Kent's wife was the voice of the parrot which Captain Crook featured on the program.

Many television markets around the country enrolled with the series for small children called *Romper Room*. Each TV teacher in every city was taught all of the same ideas for the camera and program format. Each station had its Miss Nancy, Miss Eleanor, Miss Marie, or someone. On WSIX-TV, the first teacher on *Romper Room* was Miss Norma. It was Miss Eleanor who followed her, and then came Miss Nancy, who my son said is the one that he remembers as a child.

You might remember the "live wrestling" which appeared on our local WSIX-TV station. Nick Gulas, who brought many wrestlers to the old Hippodrome, was asked to give Nashville some live wrestling on TV on Saturday nights.

On August 6, 1954, channel 5 went on the air. The station televised from the first floor of the old Life and Casualty Insurance building at Fourth and Church. The station's general manager was Mr. Tom Baker, a man I saw around when I played at WLAC radio. The owners of channel 5 were Thomas B. Baker, Jr., Alvin G. Beaman, Jr., and the Life and Casualty Insurance Company. From the early days of channel 5, you may remember Bill Jay, who played Bill J. Bumpus on the air. Bill was at channel 5 for about 33 years serving as announcer, host of children's shows, director of programming, and more.

I am sure you remember such personalities as Noble Blackwell who was host of *Night Train*, Smiling Eddie Hill, Ruth Ann Leach, and Chris Clark, who is still doing the news on channel 5.

One of channel 5's prize personalities was Oprah Winfrey, who was on the air in the 1970s. Channel 5's popular weatherman used to be Bob Lobertini. He had a children's show where the kids in the audience tried to honk Bobo's nose.

Doug Underwood, founder of the *Westview* Newspaper, was a news reporter at channel 5 when the Maxwell House Hotel burned in 1961. Doug's daughter, Paula Underwood Winters, told me that her father was not only able to report the fire. He actually pulled channel 5's equipment out on the sidewalk, and took live pictures of the hotel across the street to show in people's homes.

Channel 4 had the *Noon Show* for many years. Jud Collins was the host. Teddy Bart was on the show as a singer. Later, when Jud retired from the show, Teddy Bart became the host. The show from the start had a live band. The *Noon Show* ended in 1981.

One of the best sports shows was on Friday nights during the college football season. Jud Collins, along with Slick Welsh, gave a lot of interesting facts about the games. Also, they predicted the winners each week.

Whenever Coach Bear Bryant and the Alabama Crimson Tide came to Nashville to play Vandy, Jud and Slick usually had Bear on the TV show as their guest. I can remember how Bear always would cry about how big and mean those Vanderbilt players were, and how inexperienced and shy his little Bama boys were.

You probably saw Jud Collins, Bob Olsen, and Al Voecks announcing the news on channel 4.

Do you remember Boyce Hawkins, who was the weatherman at channel 4 before his death? Boyce also did *Adventureland* at WSM-TV. On channel 4 you might remember the *Bozo Show*, the *Bobby Lord Show*, and Ralph Emery's *Opry Almanac*.

Do you remember the TV program on channel 5 called *Woods and Water?* It was hosted by Bill Jay. That program went off the air around 1975. However, soon after that, our public TV channel put on the *Outdoor Show* with host Jimmy Holt. Those were two fine outdoor shows.

Do you remember a great science show on TV called *Mr. Wizard?* The science teacher on that show was Don Herbert.

A very popular country program was early every morning on channel 4 hosted by Ralph Emery. That show also had a live band. Do you remember Tom Grant, the Country Hams, and the Judds, who often performed on the morning show?

The Judds, when they were starting out, often appeared on that morning show with Ralph Emery, and Ralph used to call them the Soap Sisters. Naomi Judd was always talking about making soap, thus she and Wynonna were tagged the Soap Sisters.

Do you remember seeing the "Maudettes" on Ralph's early show? They were two sisters named Maude and Dorothy Paul who were always present for the morning Ralph Emery live shows.

I played six of those early morning shows, and at 4:30 AM, Maude and Dorothy served the best coffee and do-nuts you could imagine.

Old Big Band Tales

When some of us old musicians get together, we have a million stories to tell. Many of my old friends have passed away. I remember some great musicians I had the pleasure of working with such as Scobey Dill who had played on the bands of Bobby Byrne, Lou Breese, and Claude Thornhill.

I talked to Bev LeCroy on the phone the other day. He was a staff musician at WSM radio for many years. You may have heard him on *The Waking Crew* show in the mornings with another friend, Dutch Gorton, when they were billed as "The Twin Trombones." Dutch has passed away.

Until his retirement and recent death, I worked many, many jobs with Karl Garvin, a fine trumpet player who began his career at a very young age playing in Nashville with Francis Craig and His Orchestra. Karl also played with other bands of note including Joe Venuti, Jack Teagarden, Bob Chester, Sonny Dunham, and Ted Weems.

Many of you I am sure knew of Pigg & Parsons men's clothing store which closed its doors in Columbia, Tennessee during 2004 after 94 years in business. This upscale men's clothier first opened its doors in 1909 in what is now the Merrill Lynch building on the Public Square in Columbia. Later, in 1929, it moved to 117 W. Seventh Street.

Let me tell you my connection with this store. Back in the 1940s, after I returned home from the Army of World War II, I began playing again in Big Bands. Columbia's Tom Hewgley had returned from the service also along with many of us musicians who were enrolled in the music department at George Peabody College. Tom had a fine dance orchestra prior to the war when he was a music student at Middle Tennessee State College.

So, Tom again formed a good, 16-piece dance orchestra. During the war, Tom had acquired a fine book. That means he had many fine, special dance band charts or arrangements. I don't know where he got it, or who wrote it. But, the book was good.

I was hired to play in the saxophone section, and we played many prestigious locations all around Tennessee, southern Kentucky, and northern Alabama. Some of the players from his old college band were back also to join his new band, such as Scobey Dill on tenor sax, and drummer Johnny DeGeorge.

A fine Dixieland trumpeter and authority on the music of Louis Armstrong was Clay Tucker. Clay lived in Columbia and helped Tom form his band. Clay was married to the daughter of the owner of Pigg & Parsons. Clay even worked in the fine clothing store for a while. So, since I needed a tuxedo as a member of the orchestra, where do you think I bought my new tuxedo? I drove to Columbia and was fitted by my friend Clay Tucker at the fashionable Pigg & Parsons.

That was a long time ago. That band played great jobs at the Maxwell House Hotel, Hermitage Hotel, Andrew Jackson Hotel, country clubs, Vanderbilt University, Columbia Military Academy, Sewanee Military Academy, the University of the South, on and on.

Tom Hewgley with his brother, Jim, opened their Hewgley's Music Shop down on Commerce Street in Nashville. Then, Tom moved his family to Knoxville when they opened another music store there.

Many happy days were spent working with Tom's fine band. After Tom left, I went on to work in other bands. Later, I went to teach on the music faculty at Evansville College in Indiana. About the same time, my friend Clay Tucker had gone to Peabody College, received his Ph.D. degree, and later became Dean of the College of Arts and Sciences at Middle Tennessee State University.

Clay was a dean at the university the same time that I taught on the music department faculty at M. T. S. U. in 1973. Clay and I had almost 30 years of life and stories to tell each other. Clay passed away several years ago.

As I write, I am thinking of a tie-in with both Karl Garvin and Tom Hewgley. In addition to all of the fine trumpet work that Karl did, he also sang for a time with the Anita Kerr Singers. But, before then, back in 1955, Karl toured Europe with The Hilltoppers. That was a vocal group which gained a great deal of fame and popularity. The group began as students at Western Kentucky University in Bowling Green, Kentucky.

On a one-night-stand, Tom Hewgley's band played a big prom at Western Kentucky University one night. As usual, there is often some fellow who wants to sing with the band. A leader certainly can't let everyone who wants to sing take over the mike and deliver probably the worst sound you ever heard.

Well, that night at the prom, this particular fellow kept bugging Tom to let him sing with the band. Tom, who possessed one of the nicest personalities you could imagine in working with people, kept telling this fellow that we had a list of requests to play, or tried to find some other excuse or reason as to why he couldn't sing. This went on forever.

Finally, Tom told the band at one of the breaks that he guessed he was going to have to let this fellow sing something short and fast.

This fellow came to the microphone to sing. The piano man gave him an Intro. This singer knew his key, and he knew his song. We heard some really fine singing. It so happened that this fellow's name was Jimmy Sacca who later was the lead singer in The Hilltoppers who went on to record many hit recordings with Randy Wood's Dot Records. Then, Tom wished he could have hired him permanently!

Tom Hewgley and His Orchestra, c. late 1940s

Do you remember all of the New Year's Eve radio shows when every fifteen minutes the networks would have live remotes of the Big Bands? For instance, at twelve midnight, CBS, the Mutual Broadcasting System, NBC Red or Blue networks would have an announcer and engineer out at a remote location to broadcast the great bands.

On New Year's Eve in the Eastern Time Zone we might have heard Glenn Miller and His Orchestra coming from the Café Rouge of the Hotel Pennsylvania in New York City. He played there a lot. You remember the song "Pennsylvania 6-5000." That was the actual telephone number of the Hotel Pennsylvania.

Or, in the Eastern Time Zone we may have heard a remote by Gene Krupa from The Roof of the Hotel Astor on Times Square. New York was loaded with Big Bands. We could have heard Ozzie Nelson from the Lexington Hotel, Woody Herman from the Hotel New Yorker, or Charlie Barnet from the Lincoln Hotel.

And, we didn't feel like it was really New Year's Eve in New York without hearing Guy Lombardo playing "Auld Lang Syne" from the Waldorf Astoria Hotel.

Of course, from the Eastern Time Zone the remote broadcast might have been from Philadelphia, Washington D. C., or we may have heard Larry Clinton and His Orchestra playing from Frank Dailey's Meadowbrook in Cedar Grove, New Jersey.

When it was New Year's Eve in the Central Time Zone, we could have heard Kay Kyser from the Blackhawk Restaurant in Chicago, or Eddy Howard from the Aragon Ballroom.

Of course, the remote didn't have to come from Chicago. We could have heard Tony Pastor playing in the Century Room of Hotel Adolphus in Dallas, Texas, or Chuck Foster from the roof of Hotel Peabody in Memphis. I remember hearing Jan Garber coming from the Blue Room of the Roosevelt Hotel in New Orleans. Some of you may have attended the New Year's Eve dinner-dance at Nashville's Belle Meade Country Club in 1941 when Francis Craig and His Orchestra was broadcast nationally over NBC.

On New Year's Eve in the Mountain Time Zone, we might have heard a remote by Orrin Tucker playing from the Elitch's Gardens in Denver, or Charlie Barnet and His Orchestra coming from the Brown Hotel in Denver.

On New Year's Eve in the Pacific Time Zone, we may have heard Tommy Dorsey from the Hollywood Palladium, or Skinnay Ennis from the Statler Hilton Hotel in Los Angeles. We heard many remotes from time to time by Freddy Martin playing at the Coconut Grove in Los Angeles. From California we might have heard Count Basie playing at the Palomar Ballroom.

Of course, if some network wanted to get really creative, we might have heard Duke Ellington and His Orchestra playing at midnight on New Year's Eve from the London Palladium in England even before it was midnight in New York.

And, after the remotes in California, they may have sent a remote out from Honolulu to broadcast Phil Harris playing at the Royal Hawaiian Hotel on New Year's Eve.

And, to top off the greatness in broadcasting the Big Bands back in those days, we got to hear on the radio such wonderful showcases for the Big Bands as the *Camel Caravan*, the *Fitch Bandwagon*, and Coca Cola's *Parade of the Spotlight Bands*.

I am very fortunate in that I have a neighbor down the street, and another one across the street in Bellevue, who are as interested in the Big Bands as I. My neighbor, Bob Rediske, has a big collection of recordings and many books on the subject. He allowed me to borrow two books which I did not have. So, after examining his, I immediately ordered the two wonderful books on the Big Bands.

My other fine neighbor by the name of Everett Templeton who loves the Big Bands has a tremendous collection of recordings, books, and videos on the Big Bands. I have had the pleasure of observing his collection, and he has allowed me to view some of his videos of the Big Bands which I did not have. Also, Temp takes meticulous pains in cataloging every item, and listing them alphabetically.

It is a pleasure to have my love of the Big Bands shared by others.

———•———

I was pleased to see an historical marker go up off of Jefferson Street placed there by the Tennessee Historical Commission commemorating that area as part of history in jazz and rhythm and blues music.

The marker reads: "1940s-1960s Jefferson Street was one of the best-known districts of jazz, blues, and rhythm and blues."

I remember a jazz club there by the name of Club del Morocco, and one called Club Baron which today is the Elks Club on Jefferson Street. Some big stars played those clubs in years gone by including Little Richard, Fats Domino, Ray Charles, and Jimi Hendrix.

Bill "Hoss" Allen, now deceased, is still known as a legend in gospel and African-American music who was for years one of the night men at WLAC radio. Bill and I, along with many others from Vanderbilt University and Peabody College, went into the Army together during World War II.

Later, for a time, Bill was a record producer. Bill enjoyed telling this amusing story. He said that before one of his recording dates, someone said, "There is a great guitar man up at Fort Campbell. Can I bring him down for the record session?"

Bill told him that would be O. K., and he would listen to him.

In the studio the day of the session, Bill felt like he had everything ready. When he started the session, this new guitar man cut loose on some wild screeching runs and stuff that Bill didn't want. Bill "Hoss" Allen came up in the Big Bands just like I did. In fact, I met Bill Allen on a band job we played at the old Maxwell House Hotel back in 1942.

Anyway, Bill stopped the record session and tried to tell this new guitar man how to play, and exactly what he wanted. So, the session started again. This guitar man cut loose again on some wild technique. Bill stopped the session again. In fact, after a few tries, Bill just told the engineer to cut his track out. He didn't want that.

The end of the story is that Bill later learned that this new guitar man was none other than a young man by the name of Jimi Hendrix. Bill, for years after that, had to laugh, or maybe cry, because if he had known what he had, Bill "Hoss" Allen said he could have been one of the first to make a million dollars!

When Did Rock 'n' Roll Begin?

Where were you and what were you doing in 1955? Do you remember some of the things that happened back in the year 1955?

Well, for one thing, in 1955 our governor was Frank Clement elected for a second term. But, there was something significant about that term. That year the term was for four years. Before that, the governor's term was only for two years.

In 1955, President Dwight D. Eisenhower suffered a heart attack while he was golfing in Colorado. He stayed at Fitzsimons Army Medical Center in Aurora, Colorado while he recuperated.

Sir Winston Churchill retired as Great Britain's Prime Minister and was replaced by Sir Anthony Eden.

We saw the first 1955 Ford Thunderbird. However, the first one really came off the assembly line in October of 1954.

New screen star James Dean died in 1955 when his Porsche Spyder collided with another car on a California highway. Dean was 24 years old and had just completed filming his third and final major motion picture titled *Giant*. His co-stars were Rock Hudson and Elizabeth Taylor.

The AFL and CIO merged in 1955, and American Federation of Labor head George Meany became the first president of the new AFL-CIO.

Rosa Lee Parks refused to give up a seat on a Montgomery, Alabama municipal bus sparking a bus boycott. The protest marked the emergence of Martin Luther King, Jr.

as a civil-rights leader.

In 1955, Albert Einstein, one of the greatest scientific minds, died in Princeton, New Jersey.

In 1955, "Dem Bums," the Brooklyn Dodgers, won their first World Series after seven appearances. Five of those series were against the New York Yankees. Both World Series catchers won their league's MVP (Most Valuable Player) award. Roy Campanella played for the Dodgers, and Yogi Berra was the catcher for the Yankees.

Quarterback Otto Graham retired after leading the Cleveland Browns to the National Football League championship.

Some new things which appeared in 1955 were optic fiber, Play-Doh, Kellogg's Special K cereal, Disneyland in California, Crest (the first toothpaste with fluoride), and McDonald's restaurants.

Thinking of McDonald's restaurants, around 1960, Sonia and I ate our first McDonald's hamburger in Evansville, Indiana. We were attracted by the large and colorful arch above the restaurant. Also, there was a sign which read, "One million hamburgers sold." Almost a half-century later, we saw a sign on a McDonald's the other day which stated how many billions of hamburgers have been sold.

In music during 1955, we enjoyed "The Ballad of Davy Crockett, King of the Wild Frontier." Coonskin hats became famous. Do you remember Estes Kefauver, our Tennessee senator, who made the coonskin hat a Tennessee symbol?

Other hit songs of 1955 were "Dance with Me, Henry"; "Love and Marriage;" "Love Is a Many Splendored Thing;" "Moments to Remember;" and "Cry Me a River."

Popular performers with hit singles included Mitch Miller with "The Yellow Rose of Texas," Tennessee Ernie Ford with

"Sixteen Tons," Fats Domino with "Ain't That a Shame," and the Platters with "Only You."

On television we got to see *Gunsmoke, The $64,000 Question, The Secret Storm, The Honeymooners, Alfred Hitchcock Presents, Captain Kangaroo,* and *The Mickey Mouse Club.* Surely you remember how to sing M I C—K E Y—M O U S E.

It was "wunnerful" when Lawrence Welk and his music came on TV. Laugh at him if you wish, but my friends, he is still on the air today in syndication!

Among the TV shows winning an Emmy Award in that year of 1955 were *The Ed Sullivan Show,* and *You'll Never Get Rich,* my favorite show which starred Phil Silvers. Later, I think the show was called *The Phil Silvers Show.*

As for movies, *On the Waterfront* almost swept the Academy Awards with Oscars for best picture, best director who was Elia Kazan, and best actor who was Marlon Brando. Also, during 1955, Grace Kelly won an Oscar for best actress in *Country Girl.*

We saw other great actors and movies during 1955 such as Ernest Borgnine in *Marty;* Henry Fonda, James Cagney, William Powell, and Jack Lemmon in *Mister Roberts.* We saw *Oklahoma, Guys and Dolls,* and *The Blackboard Jungle.* In *The Blackboard Jungle,* Bill Haley and the Comets played "Rock Around the Clock." I told my wife after seeing that picture that I thought a new era or style of music was beginning. I had no idea at the time that it would be called "Rock 'n' Roll."

Scotty Moore, another old Tennessee musician, was invited to a 50th anniversary celebration in Memphis on July 5, 2004, as being the last surviving musician who played on a recording date of July 5, 1954, which probably began the Rock 'n' Roll era.

In Scotty's interview with *The Tennessean,* he revealed that on that July 5, 1954 record date, there were four people in the Sun Records Studio in Memphis. Besides Scotty playing guitar, there were Sam Phillips who was the owner and a producer of Sun Records, Bill Black who was the up-right bass player, and a youngster by the name of Elvis Presley.

That night, Elvis stood there in the studio and began to sing and play "That's All Right." The musicians listened, figured out the chord changes, and recorded the song five times. Two nights later, the trio cut the "B-side" of the record with a song titled "Blue Moon of Kentucky."

Scotty Moore said that the date of July 5, 1954, is the date that Rock 'n' Roll was invented. I shall accept Scotty's date as being correct.

Reflections on the Printed Word

I had not even thought about the old CORONET magazine for years and years. The other day, my son handed me a copy of the March, 1941 issue. The headline on the front of the magazine read, "Is Mussolini's Number Up? by Genevieve Tabouis."

It was fun looking at this old issue. Inside were articles such as "My Advice to Churchill" by H. G. Wells, and "Hitler Discovers America" by Rene Kraus. The magazine was similar to the *Reader's Digest* with four pages devoted to having you take a vocabulary quiz.

An order card on the inside of the magazine stated that a one year subscription was $3.00. A real bargain was to order two years for $5.00. The address on the card was N. Michigan Avenue, Chicago, Ill. Notice that this was before the two letter state abbreviations became part of the address, and there was no zip-code. Seeing old things like this really take one back to reflect on the old times.

***

I don't know whatever possessed me to start going through this big, old box of photographs and stuff before me!

The old library table, with which I had grown up since early childhood going back at least 75 or more years, had remained at my sister's home.

Recently, my sister's son was interested in taking it to his home which was fine. Before it was given to him, my sister cleaned out all of the photos, memorabilia and thousands of other things in the drawer. The contents were placed in this big box. So, now I am sitting here looking through the contents of this old box.

I have looked at many photos, at least 75 percent of which have nothing written on the backs, and I have no idea who many of the people are in the photos. I have seen many of my mother and father beginning before they married. I see other relatives which I recognize. There are many of my sister and me going back to when we were babies and beyond with our parents.

Amidst all of the photos, I ran across two old copies of *The Nashville Tennessean.* The first one was dated Thursday, July 4, 1940, and I have no idea why it was saved. The other issue was dated Saturday, March 1, 1947. I do know why that issue was saved. In fact, it is a collector's item.

First, I looked at the 1940 issue. It was interesting. The newspaper back then was called *The Nashville Tennessean* instead of the present name of the newspaper which is, *The Tennessean.* The president and publisher was Silliman Evans. The top right hand corner of the first page states: "5 Cents on street, news stands, and trains."

This issue had a large American Flag in color on the front page with a background of the entire "Declaration of Independence" printed. Well, I guess that is why I or someone in the family decided to keep it and stuck it in the old library table. I am glad.

Of course, I know why the 1947 issue of the newspaper was saved. Just above the mast head of the paper, this following statement was underlined: "Save me! I may be a collector's item some day!"

On the front page, the editor gave a lengthy explanation including this statement: "Compelled by the increasing gravity of the newsprint situation, resulting from the most acute shortage of freight cars on record in the United States and Canada, *The Nashville Tennessean*, as a temporary necessity, today prints a four-page paper which is devoid of all advertising."

How about that? Also, the issue included no editorials. It is amazing how much they got into four pages. There were some news items such as a story with the headline: "Senate Keeps Promise of Lower Income Taxes Dangling Before Public."

On the first of the four pages was Red O'Donnell's column called "Top O' the Mornin'". Red's column mentioned that Stan Kenton and His Orchestra was set for a War Memorial Auditorium engagement on April 17th.

Another item in Red's column was: "The Buford (Baby) Rays have a new daughter at their Rainbow Trail domicile." Do you remember when Baby Ray was an outstanding football player at Vanderbilt? At the time Red announced this in his column during 1947, Baby Ray was playing tackle for the Green Bay Packers.

This four-page edition included a Society section, a Stock Market Report, Death Notices, and Poultry Markets. Also, within the four pages, the edition included a listing of "Services in Nashville Churches Sunday."

There was a section on sports which included a story which began: "Georgia Tech, scoring the second upset of the day, eliminated fourth-seeded Alabama from the Southeastern Conference basketball tournament last night 43 to 40 to move into the semifinals beside Tulane, Louisiana State and Kentucky."

Yes, Tulane used to be one of the teams in the Southeastern Conference.

In spite of being just a four-page issue, the funny paper was not slighted. In case you might be wondering exactly what comics were in *The Nashville Tennessean* in this Saturday issue back in 1947, you may remember Blondie, Mary Worth, Kerry Drake, Bruce Gentry, Smiling Jack, Jane Arden, Li'l Abner, Captain Easy, Moon Mullins, Archie, Rip Kirby, and the strip called "They'll Do It Every Time."

I am only about half way through looking at the contents of this old, big box. I wonder what I shall find next?

———————— • ————————

Our son, Jeff, is an avid garage sale shopper. He actually knows how to do it properly, and come up with some very good items. Recently, he handed me some real Peabody reflections. He handed me the July, 1948 issue of *The Peabody Reflector* which he had found at a garage sale.

I graduated from George Peabody College in 1948, so seeing and reading this old issue of the magazine was of great excitement to me. Not only was my name listed as a graduate, my group picture of 1948 graduates was in the issue, and I enjoyed reading about many of my old friends in the listings whom I have not seen in more than fifty or fifty-five years.

In addition to enjoying all of that, I was reminded also of many other nostalgic items of my days so long ago. I saw a picture of a much younger Alfred Leland Crabb who had just been elected as president of the Peabody Alumni Association. I saw items about some other wonderful faculty members at Peabody back in those 1940s such as Dean Joseph Roemer, Dr. J. E. Windrow, Dr. W. H. Vaughan who was Peabody's registrar, Dr.

156

Susan B. Riley, and Dr. Irving Wolfe who was Head of the Music Department.

There were pictures of the graduation exercises and the dinners held at the close of the school year. Of the many dignitaries pictured on the stage for the graduating exercises were Mr. H. G. Hill who was a Peabody trustee, Dean W. C. Jones, President Henry H. Hill, and Dr. Felix Robb who at the time was the assistant to the president. In later years, Dr. Robb became the president of Peabody College.

At one dinner in honor of the June, 1948 graduates was pictured Governor and Mrs. Jim Nance McCord, and Peabody President Henry H. Hill.

This issue of the *Peabody Reflector* included a picture of the 1948 Peabody Demonstration School graduates. Also, there were wonderful pictures of the presentation of "Miss Peabody" with members of her court attired in beautiful dresses surrounded by the gala environment. There were pictures of President and Mrs. Hill entertaining the June graduates at their home.

This issue of the magazine went on to include pictures of the summer of 1948 college registration activities. I enjoyed reading the editorials in the magazine, and the department titled "The Mail Box."

Under the department titled "Campus News," I saw many familiar names such as Dr. Claude M. Almand who taught in the music department before I went into the Army during World War II, Dr. Hanor A. Webb who was a professor of chemistry and science education at Peabody, and Dr. Milton L. Shane who was a professor of modern languages.

Dr. J. H. Lancaster, the Peabody Librarian, had a nice write-up. By the way, his son, Jim Lancaster, played French Horn in the Nashville Symphony when I played, and Jim married a first cousin of my wife. What a small world!

In reading this old 1948 issue of *The Peabody Reflector*, I even enjoyed looking at all of the advertisements. Some of those names brought back happy memories for me. Some of those old companies might tweak your nostalgic happiness spirit, too.

You could tell it was advertising in the old days when on page two was an ad for the St. Bernard Coal Company. The company advertised "Good Coal since 1870." There were ads for Clark Hardware Company on Broadway between Fourth and Fifth Avenues, Phillips & Buttorff Manufacturing Company on Third Avenue, North which advertised Enterprise stoves, furnaces and stokers. Do you remember the old coal stokers?

I am certain ladies remember an ad by Baynham's Shoes of Distinction which was located on Sixth Avenue, North.

There was an ad for Satsuma Tea Room on Union Street, and that great Tea Room is still there today. There was an ad for White Trunk and Bag Company at 609 Church Street. Do you remember The Sweet Shop at Twenty-first and Capers Avenues near Peabody? That shop advertised "Soda, Sandwiches, Ice Cream, and Candies—We Make Our Own."

Strobel's Music Shop in the Arcade had an ad displaying their phrase "House Musical." I was interested in seeing Strobel's telephone number which was 5-6694. Do you remember when even our telephone numbers were more simple?

There was an ad for Tru-li-Pure milk by Nashville Pure Milk Company at 1401 Church Street. There was an ad for McEwen Laundry Company, established in 1881, and located at 1702 Twenty-first Avenue, South.

You probably remember when Hettie Ray's Dinner Club was located atop Nine-Mile-Hill where today sits the Wessex

Towers. Hettie Ray's was where many fraternities and sororities held their dinner-dances back in the old days. But, this ad for Hettie Ray's in the 1948 issue of *The Peabody Reflector* was for the restaurant located at 1403 Twenty-first Avenue, South and was advertising "Luncheon and Dinner with Chicken, Steak, and Country Ham."

I must really be searching for Nashville nostalgia when I get excited reading old advertisements in a magazine!

No, Nashville Is No Keeneland!

Our neighboring state of Kentucky is noted for its race horses, race tracks, breeding farms, Kentucky Derby, Churchill Downs, and Keeneland. There is even a race track in Henderson, Kentucky next to Evansville, Indiana. I guess they say it is in Kentucky. The track is on the north side of the Ohio River which should be Indiana. However, someone explained to me that the law allows the track to be located there because the "old" Kentucky boundary and the old river bed location used to be there.

No, Nashville is no race horse town. But, there is some history of race tracks associated with the Old Nashville.

Our present Centennial Park used to go by the name of West Side Park back in the 1800s. It was in West Side Park that our Tennessee Centennial was built and held in the year 1897.

Our real one-hundredth anniversary was 1896 in as much as Tennessee became the sixteenth state of the Union in 1796. Plans were made to celebrate Tennessee's 100th birthday in 1896. However, when the time came, buildings were incomplete and all of the funding was not in place. So, it was decided to postpone the opening of the Centennial Exposition for one year.

West Side Park was chosen as the grounds to build the large Exposition because the park was a 200-acre site which was our former fairgrounds and harness racing park. Of course, all Nashvillians know that the Tennessee State Fairgrounds was later, and is still, located in what used to be called Cumberland Park. Each year during the Fair week, all of us used to enjoy harness racing on the old dirt track which circled out in front of the Grandstand. The stock car races run at that same location now, but it is not the same race track.

Between the years 1970 and 1980, Metro Center was built in North Nashville close to the Cumberland River Bend, and close to downtown. Many companies located their offices there.

That Metro Center area was once the site of one of the country's best-known race tracks, the Nashville Race Course. It was sometimes called the Burns Island Tract. That race track flourished between 1828 and 1884. On October 10, 1843, I understand that the richest race in the world, the $35,000 Peytona Stakes, was run there. The winner was a Nashville horse owned by Thomas Kirkman.

General Andrew Jackson trained horses, and was a great sportsman who enjoyed racing his horses. Many years ago, Printers Alley off of the Union Street section had stables where citizens hitched their horses when they went to the courthouse. A restaurant there called The Brass Rail Stables is the spot where Andrew Jackson stabled his horses.

Back in the early 1800s, Nashville had four race tracks—one on each side of the city. One of the tracks was where Cloverbottom is located near Donelson. Due to its location near The Hermitage, this may have been the track that Andrew Jackson raced his horses.

In the late 1800s, on old Cherry Street (Fourth Avenue, North), a four-story Italianate building of brick with white marble front was erected and called Southern Turf, and was a well-known gambling spot. The building was furnished with mahogany and decorated with pier mirrors, bronze statuary, paintings, and tropical plants.

After race track betting and the sale of intoxicants were

made illegal, the old Southern Turf closed, and the building was used as offices by *The Nashville Tennessean*. That did place the publisher close to Printers Alley.

Horse racing does appear each spring in Nashville with the running of the Iroquois Memorial Steeplechase in Percy Warner Park off of Old Hickory Boulevard with the money raised going to the Vanderbilt Children's Hospital.

There was another race track off of our present Harding Road on the old Belle Meade Plantation acreage. The race track was used by the plantation in training horses such as Iroquois which was the first American bred race horse to win the English Derby. That old race track used to be roughly where our present Belle Meade United Methodist Church now sits near the corner of our present Post Road and Davidson Road.

The Belle Meade Plantation in older days was the focal point of training horses and was well known around the world. We can still tour the Belle Meade Plantation Mansion and see many interesting things about the old days, including the Carriage House on the property. Today, the Iroquois Steeplechase is the focal point of horse racing in Tennessee, but betting is illegal in our state.

The thoroughbred celebrity, Smarty Jones, who won the 2004 Kentucky Derby has connections to our Belle Meade Plantation. Many thoroughbreds were descended from three Arabians that were imported in the 1700s to England and bred to English mares. Smarty Jones is from the same line as the horses that were bred at Belle Meade Plantation, including a famous mare named Bonnie Scotland.

It proves my point that many things have their connections with our Nashville.

The Quarry

There was a place that I remember from my childhood which we simply referred to as "The Quarry."

We like to remember the good old days, but we can also remember when Nashville and Davidson County in some cases fell rather short on good sanitation.

I am sure some of you remember when many homes and schools had no indoor plumbing. There was little or no refrigeration in places. There was no air-purification or air-conditioning for many. There was no satisfactory garbage collection or disposal in some places. There was no thorough rodent or mosquito control. And, during my time, we had unprotected and smelly open trash dumps.

When I and my friends were growing up, in trying to think of something to do, we would say, "Let's go to the quarry."

This was the name we gave to a location between Paris Avenue and Cedar Lane with Belmont Boulevard to the north, and 12th Avenue to the south.

This location had three contrasting areas. There was a wooded area where we could form trails and play games as we scampered around the woods.

Also, this place had rocky cliffs on the side, and at the bottom was a small lake. When it rained heavily, there was more water in there than usual. Also, I am sure some ground water made up part of the lake aspect.

We were always trying to build a raft that we could take

out on the water. It was not only dangerous, but we never could figure out how to make a raft that would stay on top of the water and not sink!

The third and most damaging section of this area was an open city dump. Today, we could not allow such a thing. I remember that we used to get up on top of the dump away from any trees or electrical wires, and fly our kites. I have had kites fly so high that the cord would finally break, and then we had the adventure of searching several streets in the neighborhood to find the fallen kite.

The smell of the dump was horrible. We would see many rats moving all around the dump. Often a small fire would break out on the trash. I guess fires were caused by spontaneous combustion, or I have heard that when garbage begins to deteriorate into the soil, it creates methane gas. If the gas is not drained off, it causes a fire.

It was fun to watch the firemen bring in the red fire engine, string out the water hose, and put out the fire on the dump. Soon after the firemen left, the small fire would probably break out again.

A while back, I drove over to that location where the old city dump used to be. Years ago, there was no street there except for a narrow dirt road allowing access for the dump trucks to come in and unload their trash.

I found that a city street called Kirkwood Avenue runs through there now from Belmont Boulevard to 12th Avenue, South. The old city dump is filled in, and houses are built over that area. I don't know how many years ago this was done.

By slowly driving on that street, I could look between the houses and see some of the rock cliffs slopping down from the side. The area isn't the same, and thank God for that!

Nashville has come a long way with health measures and programs to protect the health of its citizens.

I give much credit to old Dr. John J. Lentz who was the Director of Health for the Davidson County Health Department. Even back in his time, he worked tirelessly to correct so many things. He fought for posting quarantine signs for contagious diseases. Children received vaccinations.

You may remember the old "No Spitting" signs posted on streetcars, sidewalks, and in other public places. Dr. Lentz worked for better sanitation and overall improvements for a healthy environment for our citizens.

Some people in the development of our city deserve a lot of appreciation from us Nashvillians.

Health care in Nashville today has become a major industry. I am glad the city named the Lentz Public Health Center on 23rd Avenue, North for and in honor of Dr. John J. Lentz. His work did not go unnoticed.

Where Did Our Governors Live?

Nashville is recognized around the world as the famous state capital of Tennessee. But, Nashville was not always the capital.

In 1796, Tennessee was admitted to the United States as the sixteenth state of the Union. John Sevier was elected governor. Knoxville was selected as the first state capital. In those early days, little thought was given to building a state capitol building, much less a residence for the governor and his family.

Our state capital kept moving. From Knoxville, it moved to Kingston for one day in 1807. The capital then moved back to Knoxville before moving to Nashville in 1812. The next move was back to Knoxville in 1817. Then, the seat of our state government moved to Murfreesboro from 1819 until 1826. Finally, On October 7, 1843, Nashville was chosen as the permanent capital of Tennessee.

But, where did our governors live?

The governors lived either in Nashville hotels or in rooming houses. Andrew Johnson was an exception. He had a home on the corner of Vine Street (Seventh Avenue) and Demonbreun Street during his first term, and another home at 58 Cedar Street (Charlotte Avenue) when he was military occupation governor.

Other governors who served between the Civil War and 1907 boarded at Nashville hotels. The most popular was the Maxwell House Hotel in room number 10 on the mezzanine floor. It was known as "The Governor's Room."

On March 11, 1907, an executive residence was finally authorized by the General Assembly of Tennessee. The fine home at 314 North Vine Street (Seventh Avenue, North) was purchased.

There used to be many fine residences in our downtown area and around the capitol building. Around the year 1921, construction was begun on the War Memorial Building. This meant the razing of several homes including this fine old mansion which had served as our first governor's residence.

After that, the state first rented the fine home at 2118 West End Avenue from Mary E. Tate, the owner. Then, in March of 1923, the state bought the West End property located across the street from Vanderbilt University.

That old mansion had been built in 1910 by Christopher T. Cheek, owner of C. T. Cheek & Co., a wholesale grocery business that Mr. Cheek ran with his sons, Leslie and Will T. Cheek. Austin Peay was the second Tennessee governor, after Governor Bob Taylor, to occupy the executive residence on West End Ave.

I have personal memories of when Governor Prentice Cooper lived there with his mother. Since Prentice was a bachelor at that time, he invited his mother to reside there and serve as the state's first lady.

I recall a memory of the late 1950s. My wife, Sonia, and I were in Chattanooga eating at a cafeteria on Main Street. I looked up and realized that Prentice Cooper was the person in line ahead of us. He was a very pleasant person.

Jim Nance McCord was the last governor to live in the executive mansion on West End Ave. The old home soon became in need of multi repairs. The house had leaks that required buckets to be placed on the floor to catch the rain water. One day the governor's wife was cooking on a wood-burning stove there when the flue broke. Soot poured out covering everything. The state began a search for other property.

The Nashville Tennessean revealed that Ridley Wills' home, which he had named "Far Hills," was for sale. National Life Insurance Company's vice-president Ridley Wills began the construction on the Georgian Colonial brick and stone house built for his wife, Jessie, in the fall of 1929.

Governor Gordon Browning met personally with Jesse Wills, the owner's son, and negotiated an excellent price for the state to pay. On January 7, 1949, Jessie Ely (Mrs. Ridley) Wills and Jesse E. Wills, acting as guardian for his father, Ridley Wills, executed a fee-simple deed conveying the home to the State of Tennessee for $120,350, which included furnishings worth $5,350.

The mansion is set on ten acres, and includes a reflecting pool, swimming pool and pool house, tennis court, putting green, greenhouse, vegetable garden, guest house and garages. The mansion has 16 rooms and 9 baths.

This residence on South Curtiswood Lane is still today only the third governor's mansion in the history of our State of Tennessee.

Nashville on Network Radio

One of my greatest loves has always been old-time radio. Back in 1941, at age 16 when I was a senior at West End High School, I began playing as a musician at WLAC radio early in the mornings. After returning from the Army of World War II, I played some more at both WLAC and WSM during the Golden Age of Radio when live music was a staple of radio broadcasting.

Today, our son, Jeff Thompson, is an announcer and producer at Big Band Radio, WAMB 1160AM, and is continuing the standards of old-time radio with his programs of good music and information over Nashville's nostalgic station.

Many of us remember the great radio dramas of the 1930s and 1940s. Even Nashville's radio station WSM produced many radio mysteries and dramas locally. When I was in junior high school, I remember WSM sent word out to students about auditions for some of those shows. I remember a girl student from my class went to the WSM studios and auditioned. She returned to inform us that she had been selected to play a young boy's part on one of the mystery shows in the afternoons.

I remember when Elmer Alley, a retired, high-standard radio broadcaster from WSM, and I had breakfast together one morning, he mentioned that when he was a student at Isaac Litton High School, he first worked at WSM radio as a sound-effects man. Also, when the need arose, he filled in on some of those radio dramas they were airing.

I gave Elmer a telephone call to ask him about those old dramas. He reminded me that one of the shows was called *Radio Patrol.* Then, I remembered that it was the one that my classmate was on in the afternoons on WSM. Elmer said that another drama was titled *Counter No. 7.* That was the story of a female clerk working in a department store. Elmer even remembered that the female lead was played by Trudy Stamper.

Elmer told me that the many wonderful radio scripts were written by an old soap opera writer who began working at WSM.

I could list many local programs which were aired back in the old days, but do you recall any of the many network programs which originated from Nashville?

Francis Craig and His Orchestra played a Sunday night program on the NBC radio network titled *Francis Craig's Sunday Night Serenade.* WSM's staff orchestra conducted by Beasley Smith aired a program called *Sunday Down South* each Sunday afternoon which was broadcast over the Lion Oil Network covered several cities. And, of course, the famous and long-lasting *Grand Ole Opry* aired many programs over the NBC radio network.

The program called *The Garden Gate* featuring the gardening specialist known as "The Old Dirtdobber" with announcer Paul Oliphant and organist Mary Elizabeth Hicks originated from Studio A at radio station WLAC, and was fed to the CBS radio network on Saturday mornings.

There were other fine network programs which originated from Nashville.

There was a musical variety show hosted by Kay Carlisle called *River Boat Revels.* The WSM staff orchestra for that show was directed by Pete Brescia, one of WSM's musical directors. Some regulars on that show were singer Joseph MacPherson, comic Minnie Pearl, The Old Timers Quartet, and announcer David Cobb. This was a 30-minute program with first broadcast over the NBC radio network in 1941.

In 1946, there was an hour program called *Opry House Matinee* that was hosted by Eddy Arnold. This country-western musical variety show had such regulars as Ernest Tubb and The Troubadours, announcer Jud Collins, The Old Hickory Singers, Rod Brasfield, Owen Bradley and his Tennesseans. This show was first broadcast in 1946 over the Mutual Broadcasting System.

There was a musical variety program called *Appointment with Music* which originated at WSM radio, and was aired over the NBC radio network. The host of the show was Snooky Lanson. Some of the regulars on the show were singer Dottie Dillard, and The Dixie Dons. Ernie Keller was the announcer, and Beasley Smith directed the WSM staff orchestra. It was a 30-minute show which had its first broadcast in 1948.

In 1952, there was a 15-minute variety show called *Home Folks* which was hosted by Owen Bradley and was aired over the CBS radio network. Regulars on that show were Ernest Tubb and The Beasley Sisters. The show was sponsored by the Quaker Oats Company.

Even later than that, *The Eddy Arnold Show* had its first broadcast over the CBS radio network in 1956. It was a variety show hosted by Eddy Arnold with regulars pianist Marvin Hughes, talented Joan Hager whom I first knew at Peabody College, and singers Dottie Dillard and Anita Kerr with whom I have worked some nice jobs. The announcer for this 30-minute show was legendary Bill "Hoss" Allen.

Nashville has always been a great radio town. WLAC and WSIX were stations with great people and live music. WSM radio probably led the way because of their great staff, studio orchestra and conductors, fine announcers, plus great broadcasting leaders as Elmer Alley, Marjorie Cooney, and Jack DeWitt who even knew how to bounce radar off the moon!

Memories of Life on the Farm

This is really a funny title for this piece, because I was not a farm boy at all. I was strictly a city boy. However, my family did visit the farm on occasions. Our cousins Mattie and Jack Phillips had a fine farm close to Watertown, Tennessee. Actually, the correct location was Cherry Valley near Shop Springs, Tennessee.

I was very young when we would visit the farm for a weekend or over-night stay. However, the farm made a definite impression on my young life. I can remember very much about that style of living. And, I loved going there.

I remember that our Daddy would get his car ready for the long journey back in the early 1930s. He would jack up the car, get under it and inspect everything. He would change the oil, take all four tires off, check the inner tubes, check the battery, the motor, and everything else. You realize that driving all the way to Cherry Valley near Watertown was quite a trip.

When my mother, daddy, sister and I approached the farm, I was designated to get out of the car, open the gates as we would come to them, and then be certain to close them back after the car went through. That was quite an important job. We couldn't allow any of the live stock to get out.

When we finally got through winding around dirt roads and arrived at Cousin Jack's house, I remember that it sat up on a hill. There was a porch that ran around three sides of the house. Down the slopes from the house were the barns, hay lofts, hog pens, and stable. The large chicken yard was on a slope the other side of the house.

During the day, my sister and I would play out in the spacious meadows. Once I can recall I made some mud pies. It hasn't been very long since I have watched my grandchildren make mud pies, too, some 65 years later.

Cousin Jack had a gentle, old horse he had named Dixie Dan. He would hook the horse up to a buggy, and we got to ride around the farm pulled by old, slow-moving Dixie Dan.

At night we washed from a big pan filled with well water. Speaking of well water, I used to love cranking the big dipper down the well and hauling up a big supply of fresh water. Once, I remember, Cousin Mattie drew up the water. When I saw her do it, I ran over to her. I guess she could tell that I was disappointed that I didn't get to haul the water up. So, she dumped the entire amount of water out on the ground, and let me do it again. I guess she knew that they had a fine supply of water at the time.

In the country, after a fine meal at the large kitchen table, they would often just throw a big, white sheet over the table, and things would be ready and waiting for us to have our next meal together.

At night we got to sleep on feather beds. You could sink down in those and get lost. Everything was so clean, and smelled so fresh. I loved it.

The next day, after a fine breakfast, I would go around and help do some farming. Of course, they had to milk the cows, feed the sheep, goats, horses, chickens, and slop the hogs. Sorry, folks, but that is what farmers did to the hogs!

I remember one trip to Cherry Valley in particular. Daddy was not really sure how to get out and back on the road to Nashville. A Greyhound bus happened to come along marked "Nashville." So, Daddy just decided to follow that bus.

That turned out to be rather difficult though. First of all, the bus was going too fast. Also, on the dirt roads a cloud of dust was thrown up so that it was hard to stay behind the bus anyway.

No, I definitely was never a farm boy, but I can remember some of the interesting parts of that life-style.

For me, and the rest of my family, it was back to the city. We would go shopping downtown. We would buy our groceries at the grocery store. We just bought one quart of milk at a time. We could buy ice for our ice box at a near-by ice house.

We walked back to Clemons School on the next school day. We may have bought some produce from a horse-drawn market wagon which would come through the neighborhood. You recall how the driver would yell, "Red ripe tomatoes, Irish potatoes, tender field corn, and home-grown cantaloupes," or something like that. In the city, we could even go to a movie if we wanted.

I had wonderful experiences when we visited the farm. Sometimes things got a little hectic in the stress of the city life. They are two entirely different styles of living.

The next time you see an old farmer with rough and worn hands, you salute him. He has been closer to the earth of God's creation than most of us ever will in pulling out from the dirt the life-giving resources for us all.

Nashville Needs A Breakfast Club

No, I'm not talking about FOOD. I am talking about old RADIO. Station WLAC at one time had a "Breakfast Club" type program in the mornings at the old Noel Hotel. The Noel was across Church Street from the old Third National Bank building, atop of which was radio station WLAC.

Of course, the mother of all "Breakfast Clubs" was heard nationally over the Blue Network and then the ABC radio network from 1933 until 1968. That was a very successful effort for a radio program which went simply by the name *The Breakfast Club* starring Don McNeill.

For many years, we Nashvillians and citizens everywhere could arise each morning to hear real happiness during our breakfast. Maybe you remember some of the many entertainers on the radio program.

For a while, Marian and Jim Jordan were heard in their comedy skits as "Toots and Chickie." If you recognize their names, you know that later Marian and Jim were known nationally on their own show called *Fibber McGee and Molly*. Also, on *The Breakfast Club* we heard Bill Thompson with his Wallace Wimple voice who later also moved over to *Fibber McGee and Molly*.

There were some good singers on the show over those many years. Do you remember Dick Teela, Jack Owens, The Merry Macs, Clark Dennis, Annette King, Jack Baker, Johnny Johnston, The Dinning Sisters, Johnny Desmond, and The Vagabonds?

The *Breakfast Club* ran for about 35 years, so you can imagine how many entertainers were in and out of Chicago on that show. In fact, our own "Homer and Jethro" joined the show in 1952.

Another great character on *The Breakfast Club* was Fran Allison. She sang too, but mostly I remember her playing the endearing character "Aunt Fanny" delivering her hilarious lines. After her years on this show, I am sure you remember early television when Fran Allison moved to television and was seen in a great, early puppet program with Burr Tillstrom called *Kukla, Fran, and Ollie.*

There was a live band on *The Breakfast Club* shows. There were a number of band leaders over the years which maybe you never heard of; however, you may recall Don McNeill referring to them. There were Walter Blaufuss, Harry Kogen, Joe Gallicchio, Rex Maupin, and Eddie Ballantine.

There were many announcers on the show at various times. Do you remember hearing Durward Kirby at one time? You may remember when Durward Kirby worked with Garry Moore on *The Garry Moore Show.* Also, Durward announced on a radio soap opera called *Lone Journey.* And, maybe you remember Durward Kirby as the announcer on a quiz show called *Two for the Money* which featured the quizmaster-comic Herb Shriner.

Don McNeill and his wife went on a second honeymoon in 1948, and the two people that subbed for Don on *The Breakfast Club* were Allen Prescott and Jack Paar. Sorrowfully, Jack Paar just died at the end of January, 2004.

The Breakfast Club was a live, free-wheeling show, and no one knew exactly what might happen. Other terms used could be "off the cuff," or "they just winged it." Don McNeill got the idea to divide the hour-long show into four equal segments. Don would refer to them as "The four calls to breakfast."

In the first quarter, McNeill interviewed people from the audience. Also, during this first quarter, the orchestra offered some brisk "waker-uppers" as Don would say. In the second call to breakfast, Don had a "Memory Time," and presented a reading of a sentimental verse. Also, Don introduced "Prayer Time" during World War II. This feature was so popular that it continued after the war. Often in this segment came "Hymn Time." Also, a segment was called "Sunshine Shower." Don urged listeners to drop lines of cheer to people in hospitals, orphanages, and homes for the elderly.

The third call to breakfast was "March Time." I can remember when the orchestra played a rousing march and Don would invite all of the cast members and some of the audience to march around the breakfast table. The *New Yorker* magazine called Don's audience to be "the solid citizens, the churchgoers, the butcher, the baker, and the candlestick maker."

In 1946, Don asked his listeners to share a meal with unfortunates in war-torn Europe. Forty tons of food were collected.

The fourth call to breakfast, the last 15 minutes of the show, was for "Inspiration Time" when Don presented a message or poem designed to lift the spirits of the downcast.

The Breakfast Club combined unabashed sentiment, human interest, band music, and song. I don't guess the show would go over today, much less run for 35 years which it did then. But, somehow I believe I would still listen to it as I did when I was a kid.

In Don McNeill's own words, he said: *"The Breakfast Club* is a get-together time for all of us who smile before breakfast, and then can't break the habit all day long."

Nostalgia Surrounds Nashville

Greater Nashville has been a big part of our lives through the years. There are many things and locations in our surrounding area which lift our nostalgic spirit.

We travel quite a lot on U.S. Highway 31 through Franklin and Spring Hill to Columbia, Tennessee when we visit our daughter, Lee Anne, her husband, Jeff Parsley, and our five grandchildren.

Across from the Saturn Corporation's plant is the Rippavilla Plantation. The home, built in 1852, has been restored and features many of the original family's heirlooms and furnishings.

Columbia, Tennessee has earned the reputation of being the "Antebellum Homes Capital of Tennessee." President James K. Polk's home is there. It was built by his parents in 1816. This is the home where Polk began his legal and political career.

Among the many antebellum homes in Columbia is the Athenaeum Rectory, built in 1837 in a Moorish-Gothic architectural design which I find enjoyable just to look at. In 1852, it became the home to the Columbia Athenaeum School for Young Ladies. It was a well-respected girls' school for more than fifty years. Girls were taught a wide range of quality courses, including mathematics, physics, science, and business.

What is very interesting is that now each summer, the present owners and operators of the restored structure conduct a nostalgic remembrance of the old Athenaeum Girls' School.

For one full week each July, young ladies ages 14 to 18 from all over the country dress in authentic 19th century costumes and study the same courses in etiquette, penmanship, art, music, and social graces as did the young ladies of 150 years ago. Older ladies are offered a condensed two-day version of the school each May.

Columbia Athenaeum School for Young Ladies

The Carter House in Franklin, Tennessee on Columbia Avenue is an interesting place to visit, especially for the Civil War buffs. This house played a big role in the Battle of Franklin.

About five miles from there, the Carnton Mansion also played a part in the Civil War. From the back porch of the mansion, you can see the only privately owned Confederate cemetery in the United States.

Do you remember the Monkees' big hit "The Last Train to Clarksville?" Some people say that song was inspired by the

L & N Railroad Station in Clarksville, Tennessee. The once-busy depot built in 1890 is now a museum and art gallery.

Do you remember old Dunbar Cave near Clarksville? I have played many dance jobs in the mouth of that huge cave. There was a rock formation there which served as a perfect bandstand. All of the bands from Nashville played dates there including Francis Craig, Owen Bradley, Tommy Knowles, Tom Hewgley, and others. In fact, I guess every musician back in the old days played Dunbar Cave.

For a number of years, Roy Acuff owned the property. He did many country music shows there as well as the Saturday night dances. Today, owned by the State of Tennessee, the area is 110 scenic acres of history and legend called the Dunbar Cave State Natural Area.

In Gallatin, Tennessee there is Trousdale Place which was the home of Tennessee Governor William Trousdale. He served as governor from 1849 to 1851. The home has been restored and contains period antiques.

In Castalian Springs in Sumner County, what may be the largest log structure ever erected in Tennessee still stands. Wynnewood was built in 1828 as a stagecoach inn and mineral springs resort. By 1840, a row of cottages adjoining the inn had been built. Some of the logs, mostly oak and walnut, are 32 feet long. Wynnewood is now owned by the State of Tennessee.

Nashville and Tennessee are unique places to live.

Through the Decades

Every decade in our history has its happy moments as well as its sad memories.

In taking a mental trip back over several decades, what words or phrases come to your mind when thinking about the 1930s?

I can think of Adolph Hitler, The Great Depression, F. D. R., the New Deal, W. P. A., the birth of Social Security, the matinee hop at the downtown Y. W. C. A., jitterbugging, banana splits, and Candyland.

I can think about the gigantic East Nashville tornado, the United States Post Office was built on Broadway, Berry Field was dedicated, our Davidson County Courthouse was dedicated, and the Tennessee State Supreme Court building was built.

When thinking of the 1940s, my mind has to think of "the war years," windows displaying flags signifying persons from that home in the Armed Forces, gold stars, rationing of sugar, butter, meat, gasoline, and tires. I think of Victory gardens, buying U. S. War Bonds, and saving tinfoil. *Your Hit Parade* on radio even advertised their Lucky Strike sponsor with the phrase "Lucky Strike green has gone to war."

Ladies gave up wearing nylons as the material was needed to make parachutes. We heard about air raids. During the war years, do you remember the terms Lend Lease, Marshall Plan, and the Atlantic Charter?

During the 1940s, busses replaced streetcars in Nashville,

we saw the first ballpoint pens, drive-up banks, and 33 1/3 RPM record albums. Many veterans were going to school on the GI Bill of Rights.

The Nashville Symphony Orchestra was established. A two-percent sales tax was enacted. Also, we could buy four records for 99 cents and have a party in the basement.

What do we think of when reminiscing about the 1950s? In the early 1950s, school segregation was declared unconstitutional. Nashville began to set up a program for civil rights legislation and integration.

The Women's track team at Tennessee State University began competing in the Olympics under legendary coach Ed Temple which would see many gold medals honor our great city.

I remember that Thanksgiving Day in 1950 was the first Clinic Bowl played at the Vanderbilt stadium.

Many thought of the 1950s as still being in the Golden Age of Radio and still in The Golden Age of the Big Bands. Television came to Nashville. Some theatres had to give away money and dishes in hopes of getting an audience into the show palaces.

Harry Truman was president. Then, General "Ike" Dwight D. Eisenhower served as president in our country's prosperity from 1953 until 1961. The economy was recovering. Of course, we had the Korean War and the McCarthy witch hunts for communist spies.

The 1950s saw the hydrogen bomb, the Salk polio vaccine, NASA, and the addition of Alaska and Hawaii as our 49th and 50th states.

We went to drive-in movies, Elvis had teen-aged girls going ga-ga, Russia's Sputnik launched our race to the moon, the Life & Casualty building was completed at the corner of

Fourth and Church, Billy Graham held his first Crusade in Nashville at Dudley Field, and the Vanderbilt football team played in the Gator Bowl and beat Auburn.

In the 1960s, a young president served our country. Then, on November 22, 1963, we saw President John F. Kennedy assassinated. Later, his brother, Robert F. Kennedy, was assassinated. A distinguished African-American shared a dream. Dr. Martin Luther King, Jr. was assassinated, also.

In the 1960s, our old, historic Maxwell House Hotel burned, the Municipal Auditorium was built, Cuba became communistic, and the war in Vietnam escalated. President Lyndon B. Johnson decided not to run for a second term. Richard Nixon became president. 100 Oaks Shopping Center opened as a fully enclosed mall.

In the 1960s, we experienced G. I. Joe dolls, Beatle mania, instant replay on television in sports, and we got to laugh at *Our Miss Brooks* and *Who Do You Trust.* In 1969, Neil Armstrong walked on the moon.

We enjoyed reading "Peanuts" in the funny paper as well as "Miss Peach," "Grandma," "Judge Parker," and "Nancy."

Our Metropolitan Government of Nashville-Davidson County was officially established.

In the 1970s, Nixon was re-elected president as events around Watergate surfaced. The Vietnam War continued until 1975. Roe vs. Wade legalized abortion and controversy was unleashed. The voting age was lowered to 18. In 1974, President Nixon resigned from office.

Opryland USA theme park opened as did the Opryland Hotel which added excitement to our lives and brought many tourists to Nashville. Rivergate Mall opened as Nashville's second fully enclosed mall. 100 Oaks Mall was declared the first. However, I like to think of The Arcade as being our first fully enclosed mall.

The 1980s placed Ronald Reagan in the White House. Cuban refugees began arriving. AIDS was spreading. The Challenger exploded before our horrified eyes as we watched television.

Since the 1980s, Nashvillians have been enriched by the presence of the Tennessee Performing Arts Center. Our old Union Station became the Union Station Hotel. Our new International Airport was finished.

Starwood Amphitheatre opened, and Candyland at Seventh and Church closed.

We have memories both good and bad. But, somehow our minds seem to filter out the hard times. We remember the great times, the happy times, and the things that we can laugh about.

I enjoy thinking about NASHVILLE NOSTALGIA.

When Shopping Meant Downtown Nashville

An eclectic collection of sidewalk guests
busily on their mysterious errands

As I have spoken around town to clubs and churches about "Nashville Nostalgia," I have learned that the topic that interests and excites many people is looking back at the old days when Fifth, Sixth, Seventh Avenues, Church Street, and the surrounding area downtown was our shopping center. This period of time was before neighborhood shopping malls.

Back in the old days, the memorable streetcars took us to an exciting world which we called downtown. Downtown was the world of department stores, many restaurants and movie theatres. Fifth Avenue was the Five & Ten Cent Store area. The Arcade downtown was really our first covered mall. Many Nashvillians worked in the offices and buildings in what we called "downtown."

A journey into this old Nashville meant meeting and greeting, shopping and eating.

To help bring back some wonderful nostalgia of our beloved Nashville, I want you to walk with me around old downtown Nashville so that all of us can remember and feel the nostalgic spirit, visualize the sights, sounds, aromas, tastes, and re-live some wonderful memories of our downtown shopping area.

Let us remember what downtown was like during the 1940s, 1950s, and 1960s.

When There Were No Shopping Malls circa 1940s

Let's take a walk on downtown Church Street, and remember some of the things we saw when some of us were growing up in Nashville back in the late 1930s and 1940s. Many of you will remember the huge throng of humans jamming the sidewalks amid the hustle, bustle, and competition.

Starting at the corner of Fifth Avenue and Church Street, let's walk toward the west remembering some of the sights. Visualize in your mind, the old Presbyterian Church at the corner of Fifth and Church which stood during the Civil War and still stands today. That building was the First Presbyterian Church before the congregation moved out to its present location at the corner of Tyne Boulevard and Franklin Pike. Today, that historic building at Fifth and Church is the Downtown Presbyterian Church.

Now, cross the street heading west, and in the old days, we would be standing in front of the Jackson Building at that particular corner. The several floors of the building were occupied with offices of many types. But, I especially remember the street level which was Shacklett's Cafeteria. We ate there many times.

Walking on we would see Candy's Inc. where we drooled over the various confectionaries. Still moving west on Church Street, we would be at the entrance of the old Princess Theatre. There we could enjoy movies as well as a stage show still hanging on to the old Vaudeville days. I can remember seeing

Fifth Avenue

Blackstone the Magician. This was the father of the Blackstone in more modern times. I remember Brent Wood, a fine harmonica player. He was my father's favorite. We saw acrobats, jugglers, comedians, dancers, singers, even the Rhythm Boys were booked into the Princess. You may remember one of The Rhythm Boys by the name of Bing Crosby. Jack Benny and Donald O'Connor played the Princess in years gone by.

Do you remember the Kay Jewelry Company and Nashville Trunk and Bag Company between Fifth and Sixth Avenues? Also, there was the Florsheim Shoe Shop.

Moving on down, we are now in front of the McKendree Methodist Church which has been at that same location for many years. Also, in that block was Buhl Optical Company.

Then, we come to the corner where we see the twelve-story Warner Building. This, of course, was before the Tennessee Theatre was built. Later, the Warner Building was renamed the Sudekum Building. Even after that, the building was called the Tennessee Building. Today, that corner is taken up by the fashionable Cumberland Apartments.

Now, we are at Sixth Avenue, so let's turn around, walk back to Fifth and Church and see what is on the other side of the street.

On the corner of Fifth Avenue (old Summer Street) and Church Street back during the Civil War period, a hotel called the St. Cloud House occupied that location. In fact, that corner is still called St. Cloud's Corner.

We remember that corner as being the Cain-Sloan Company. It was later that Cain-Sloan moved across the street to another corner of Fifth and Church.

Harvey's Department Store

Walking west on Church Street from Cain-Sloan you may remember the Peiser Millinery Company. Also, there was the Linen and Baby Shop, and Jean's Hosiery Shop.

Do you remember that a Warner Drugstore was in that block? Lebeck Brothers department store was there in 1940. Also, in that block was Chandler Boot Shop and a couple of apparel shops at some time.

In the early 1940s, Harvey's great department store moved into the old Lebeck's space. Harvey's soon became a giant department store expanding to include the entire block between Fifth and Sixth Avenues which featured its escalators, the third floor Monkey Bar with real live monkeys, the wild colored carousel horse figures all around, the real carousel which children could ride, and the Downstairs Dinette which later served the fantastic apple pie which had moved to Harvey's after the closing of Kleeman's Restaurant. It was "fun to shop at Harvey's."

Look at that block of downtown today, and it is not too exciting. It certainly doesn't have that charm of sidewalks covered with shoppers, friends yelling at each other as they meet, and looking in each other's sacks to see what they had bought.

———◆———

Let's continue walking west on Church Street from the corner of Sixth and Church.

On the south side of Church back in the 1940s, do you remember when Joy Floral Company was on the corner? The building at the corner was the Watkins Building. It was the home of the famous Watkins Institute.

Watkins Institute has a great history. Samuel Watkins was a major contractor in early Nashville. At his death in 1880, Watkins gave this piece of property at Sixth and Church plus $100,000 to the city as an endowment with the stipulation that it was to serve as a pioneer school for adult education. Watkins

Institute has been in continuous operation since 1885.

Watkins Institute has now relocated at the old Fountain Square area in the former, spacious movie multiplex in Metro Center. And, the name of the old Institute today has been changed to Watkins College of Art & Design.

But, let's get back to the block between Sixth and Seventh Avenues before the Church Street Center was built in that block, which was there before our Nashville Public Library was built and takes up that whole block today.

In that old Watkins Building were also other office spaces. For instance, the Nashville Electric Service was in that building as well as the Electric Power Board of Nashville. I can remember as a child walking down the long corridor with my mother to pay our electric bill each month. Back then, we just called it our "light bill."

Moving west on Church Street we had Flagg Brothers Shoes, and White Trunk and Bag Company. Do you remember the small, thin building there which was the Church Street branch of the American National Bank? That was my bank for a while. Also, in that block was Sam Small Jewelry Company.

Walking on, we are now at the Vendome Building. There were many offices above the street level such as life insurance offices, dentists, chiropractors, and even a tailor. But, the biggest remembrance within our nostalgic spirit would have to be the brilliant lights and marquee of the Loew's Vendome Theatre. It sat right at the foot of Capitol Boulevard, the street heading up toward our Tennessee State Capitol building.

The old Loew's Theatre still had box seats at each side of the auditorium reflecting the days when the theatre embraced great stage productions. Later, as a movie theatre, I remember the long lobby which displayed many posters of the great MGM movie stars featured at the theatre. I remember such stars as

Clark Gable, Lionel Barrymore, Barbara Stanwyck, Robert Taylor, Frank Morgan, Judy Garland, Ann Rutherford, and I saw every one of the "Andy Hardy" pictures starring Mickey Rooney, Lewis Stone, Fay Holden, and Cecilia Parker at the Loew's Theatre.

After I wrote a *Westview* Newspaper column about our old downtown shopping district, I received a wonderful, four-page, handwritten letter from Edith Trotter in which she was inspired to tell me many of her nostalgic memories. Edith is a native Nashvillian who grew up in the Sylvan Park area of West Nashville. Edith mentioned that she remembers the LaVogue Beauty Salon which was upstairs in the Vendome Building where her Mom always got her hair done by owner Nona Crews.

Continuing to walk on Church Street, we would have seen Goldners Jewelers, Joe Morse clothing company, and Meyer Jewelry Company. Also, in that block between Sixth and Seventh were optometrists, a hat cleaner, and Harold L. Shyer Jewelers. And, "if you don't know your diamonds, know your jeweler. And, if Harold says it's so, it's so!"

There was a narrowly built Krystal in that block. I can still visualize the Krystal ball displayed outside, and we could watch the cake do-nuts being made in Krystal's front window. Also, there was the T & K Sandwich Shop, and a beauty shop in that area.

Then, when we would arrive at the corner of Seventh and Church, we wouldn't keep walking. Instead, we would walk directly into Candyland and get a chocolate sundae, chocolate soda, and even sandwiches, candy, you name it.

During the 1940s, many of you remember that military maneuvers came to this part of Tennessee. Hundreds of thousands of military personnel were trained within the borders of our Volunteer State. One reason was that the nature of Tennessee's terrain with a variety of landscapes offered a wonderful practice grounds for military personnel to learn their needed skills.

The Mecca Restaurant sat on the corner across from the Castner-Knott Dry Goods Company, and was well-attended by our service personnel. Tennessee and Nashville had thousands of service men and women coming through because of those maneuvers, our Thayer General Hospital, the Army Air Corps Classification Center, and Smyrna Air Base near by. Thousands of World War II veterans have a kind remembrance of our Nashville on the Cumberland Bluffs, and the hospitality of The Mecca Restaurant.

Now, let's walk back to Sixth Avenue and Church Street and walk down the other side of the street. On that corner of Sixth and Church, do you remember the United Cigar Store? That side of Church Street had a Lerner Shop, and other dress shops and shoe stores.

After crossing over Capitol Boulevard, we first would come to Armstrong's, a nice women's clothing store. The rest of that block up to Seventh Avenue was Castner- Knott Dry Goods Store.

———•———

Let's not slight Capitol Boulevard which in its day has seen parades following World War I and World War II. More recently, the street had been blocked off as part of our Summer Lights Festival.

Many great businesses have enjoyed the old Capitol Boulevard location over the years. Do you remember such places as Heald Steak Shop Restaurant, the rear entrance of Joseph Frank & Son, Goodie Eat Shop, and the Knickerbocker Theatre? That narrowly built theatre extended from Capitol Boulevard to Sixth Avenue with box offices on both streets.

You probably remember many other places on Capitol over the years. There were Weinberg's Ladies Wear, Friedman Tailors, and Grace's, a great shop for ladies.

Of course, up at the corner of Capitol and Union Street, we still have the back side of the historic Hermitage Hotel, and on the other side of Capitol we then had the back side of the old YMCA Building where a hotel now sits. That old YMCA Building housed eight floors of dormitories, gymnasiums, and offices. The old Nashville Business College was in that building as well as the YMCA School of Law.

Let's continue our walk west on Church Street remembering some of the things that were there during the 1940s.

Walking from Seventh and Church, we remember Tinsley's, a wonderful ladies ready-to-wear store. Mills Bookstore was in that block as well as a Sherwin-Williams Paint Store, and Domenick Restaurant.

Walking on toward Eighth Avenue, we would come to my old hangout, Claude P. Street Piano Company. I began taking music lessons there when I was twelve years old. The street floor was a large display of pianos. Mr. Jack Wright was the salesman and store manager. Also, I remember seeing the kind Mr. Claude P. Street every time I was there.

After I signed in and paid 50 cents for my music lesson at Street's, I went to the elevator which I would operate myself.

194

That was always fun to close the elevator door, turn the handle, and go up to the third floor where my teacher's studio was located.

I remember that Elizabeth B. Combs Dance Studio was on that floor, also. I sometimes would enjoy watching them while I sat outside to wait for my lesson. My teacher was Mr. Fred Murff. Another teacher was Lisbeth Smith. She was the sister of Beasley Smith who was one of the musical directors of the staff orchestra at WSM radio. After a while, Fred Murff and Lisbeth Smith married, and they were very good friends of mine for many years to come.

Let's walk on. Next door to Street's was Zibart's Bookstore. Then, there was an alley, and next stood the Paramount Theatre with its large sign above the marquee looking toward the sky spelling out in large letters PARAMOUNT.

Finally, the next and last building before Eighth Avenue was the old Sears and Roebuck Company. That building was other things over the years after Sears, and today it is an office building.

All of downtown back in the old days (circa 1940s) was business, shopping, restaurants, and entertainment. Now, let's go back and walk down the other side of Church Street.

Let's start at Seventh and Church in front of the old Bennie Dillon Building and the old Doctor's Building. Both of those old structures still stand there today. Both of those buildings used to be full of movement and excitement as people swarmed to the various doctors, dentists, and other offices.

In that block was Massey Surgical Supply and Nashville Surgical Supply. The Board of Missions for the Methodist Church was in that block.

I remember that a Wilson-Quick Pharmacy was in that block when I was a kid. The drugstore had a wonderful lunch counter and soda fountain. On many Saturdays, Elva, my sister, and I used to go to that lunch counter for something to eat before we went to a movie. I remember that I always got a ham salad sandwich and a chocolate soda. Then, off we would go to the Paramount, Loew's, or Knickerbocker Theatre to see a movie. However, first we may have dropped by a Five & Ten Cent Store on Fifth Avenue, or The Peanut Shop in the Arcade to get a supply of jelly beans, candy, or hot roasted peanuts to take into the movie theatre.

In that block between Seventh and Eighth Avenues was the Church Street branch of the Broadway National Bank, and a branch of the Model Laundry. At the corner of Eighth and Church was the old Tulane Hotel.

But, before we stop walking around downtown, I think we should look in on old Fifth Avenue where everyone came to greet and meet, shop and eat around 1940.

The hustle and bustle of old Fifth Avenue had great stores like Cain-Sloan at one corner and Loveman's at the other. We had four Five & Ten Cent Stores. The last time I walked down Fifth Avenue, the old Kress Building was vacant. At the top of that old five-story building, I could still see the large gold letters spelling KRESS.

Back in the old days, on the west side of Fifth Avenue starting at Church Street we had the Cain-Sloan Company. This is where it was before Harvey's took in the whole block of Church Street, and also before Cain-Sloan moved across Church Street, re-locating from the corner of Fifth Avenue down to the McKendree Methodist Church. Of course, Cain-Sloan and Harvey's both are now gone.

196

Also, on the west side of Fifth Avenue, the Five & Ten Cent Stores were W. T. Grant, F. W. Woolworth, McLellan's, and S. H. Kress stores.

On that block of Fifth Avenue between Church and Union there were other small shops, too. I remember a hat shop, the Fox dress shop, and Baker's shoe store. At the corner of Fifth Avenue and Union Street was the lovely Loveman, Berger & Teitlebaum Department Store. We just called it Loveman's. Today at that corner is The Five Hundred and One Union Building.

On the east side of Fifth Avenue in this block between Church Street and Union Street, starting up at the Church Street corner, I can remember a tobacco shop, an Orange Bar which sold fruit juices, a Krystal, and optometrist E. Lee Bennett's office.

There were two movie theatres on that side of the street. We had the Rex Theatre and the Fifth Avenue Theatre. Most of that area today is taken up by the Sun Trust Bank Building.

Next to the Arcade, which really is an enclosed shopping mall, there was always a drugstore during my time. Even today, there is a Walgreens Drugstore next to the Arcade.

There were some other shops on that side of Fifth Avenue between the Arcade and Union Street. There was a dress shop, a linen shop, a hat shop, and a Family Booterie.

Back in my time, the old streetcars took us to an exciting world which we called downtown. It was the world of department stores, Five & Ten Cent Stores, lunch places, theatres, and people. Boys made sure that their hair was combed. Girls were so neat in their nice dresses, dainty little hats, and wrist-length white gloves.

I can remember old Fifth Avenue and smile. In thinking back to those old days, I miss the screaming when we saw someone we knew, pulling something out of a sack to show a friend what we had just bought, deciding where to go to get a soda, and maybe buying tickets to a movie.

A Saturday journey into this old world meant greeting and meeting, shopping and eating. In thinking back to those old days, I miss my friends calling me and saying, "I'll meet you on Fifth Avenue!"

Another Walk Back in Time circa 1950s

Only a decade later, our old downtown was beginning to age and show some change. Of course, all of the change wasn't bad. For instance, we still had some wonderful places to eat, there were still some theatres downtown, our Five & Ten Cent Stores were still on Fifth Avenue, and Harvey's had begun to develop an outstanding department store for Nashville.

In the 1950s, some of the shopping had begun to thin out on Church Street between Fifth and Sixth Avenues. We still had the historic McKendree Methodist Church. Vaudeville at the Princess Theatre had left us, but look what we have here! Across the alley from the church stands one of the finest theatres Nashville ever had. The Tennessee Theatre came on the scene for Nashvillians to enjoy.

On the night of the theatre's Grand Opening, February 28, 1952, we experienced Hollywood type flood lights and a parade. I played in a band outside of the theatre as guest movie stars arrived in convertibles. I remember the guest actors invited were Lex Barker, Arlene Dahl, Virginia Gibson, Phyllis Kirk, Jack Wesson, and Gordon McCrae. The movie at the Grand Opening was a musical comedy titled *About Face*.

Down at the corner of Church and Sixth Avenue, we still had the 12-story Warner Building. Also, the Musicians' Union office, where I had become a member about ten years earlier, was still on the sixth floor. In fact, the offices had expanded to numbers 600 and 602.

Harvey's Department Store began expansion which eventually would become a forceful and thriving department store with many advanced ideas in marketing. Harvey's was the first in Middle Tennessee to install escalators. The decorated window displays at Harvey's during Christmas time were the talk of the town.

Harvey's decorated the store with their trademark of horses and other parts of a carousel painted red, purple, and all wild colors. The original carousel horses came from the old carousel in Glendale Park which closed in 1932. The old, dismantled Glendale Park carousel was found in a barn according to Mr. Fred Harvey, Jr., and Harvey's Department Store bought the parts. What a flood of nostalgic happiness deluged my mind when I learned that the old carousel that my sister and I rode in Glendale Park was the same as we were seeing in Harvey's Department Store.

Walking on west on Church Street back in the 1950s, we found Joy Floral Company on the corner of Sixth and Church. There was an H. G. Hill Grocery Store in that block. The Watkins Building was still there supporting the historic Watkins Institute which offered education to adults and continuing education students. In the Watkins Building there were many offices. We paid our light bills at the Nashville Electric Service offices in that building.

Also, on that side of Church Street we had Kay Jewelry Company, and White Trunk & Bag Company. Do you remember banking at the First American National Bank branch on Church Street? The Vendome Building was still there with its many office tenants, and our Loew's Vendome Theatre was still showing fine movies.

Other stores in that block were Weinstein Jewelry Company, Baker's Shoe Store, Meyer Jewelers, Flagg Brothers

Shoes, and Harold L. Shyer Jewelry store.

The Krystal was still serving hamburgers, or you could eat at the E & H Sandwich Shop next door. Candyland was still on the corner of Seventh and Church.

On the other side of Church Street between Sixth and Seventh, we had the National Shirt Shop, Barton's selling women's clothing, as well as Chesters. There was Holiday's Shoe Store, and Armstrong's women's apparel where women loved to shop. From there on to Seventh Avenue was the fine Castner-Knott Dry Goods Company.

There was still wonderful shopping between Seventh and Eighth Avenues. On one side of Church Street we had Tinsley's of Nashville which was attractive to women shoppers. We had Bell's Booterie, Dailey's Men's Clothing, Nick & Domenick Restaurant, and Joe Morse Company for men's clothing. There was a branch of the Third National Bank, and Zibart's Bookstore. We still had the Paramount Theatre, and the end of the block at Eighth Avenue was Sears and Roebuck in 1950.

On the other side of Church Street between Seventh and Eighth Avenues, you will remember Chandler Boot Store, the Bennie-Dillon Building, Massey Surgical Supply, the Doctor's Building, my great old Wilson-Quick Drugstore where I visited the lunch counter before going to a movie, Nashville Surgical Supply, and Gus Mayer Company.

I can remember the Broadway National Bank branch there. Then, there were Gaines Shoe Company, Model Laundry, and Weinberger's selling women's clothing. The great, old Tulane Hotel was torn down in 1956.

———◆———

Capitol Boulevard was often changing. But, you probably remember the Goodie Eat Shop, and Zanini's Restaurant on Capitol. Starting down at Church Street and Capitol Boulevard, do you remember Joseph Frank & Sons had a rear entrance on Capitol? The Knickerbocker Theatre was still there, but not for long. There was a rear entrance on Capitol Boulevard of the Youth Shop.

On Capitol Boulevard there was a district office of the National Life & Accident Insurance Company, and Sonotone of Nashville was there selling hearing aids. Mrs. Virginia Walker Antiques was located on Capitol as was the American Textile Machines Corporation.

There was the Capitol Boulevard Building with its many offices. A Western Union Telegraph branch office was there, and Grace's rear entrance was on Capitol Boulevard.

———•———

Old Fifth Avenue was still perking, but not quite like the old days. However, it was still going. Up at Fifth and Church, where today we have the Sun Trust Bank Building taking up a good bit of the area, there was still a Cigar Store at the corner plus the fruit juice place which was called California Orange Bar.

Dr. E. Lee Bennett still had his office there next to the Krystal. Also, there was a Russell Stover Candy store in that block, plus clothing stores, Nashville School of Beauty Culture, Goldner's Jewelry store, Banks Olshine store, and Brooks clothing store for men.

The Rex Theatre and the Fifth Avenue Theatre were still there, and Walgreens Drugstore was next to the Arcade.

Up at Fifth and Church was Cain-Sloan Company at St. Cloud's Corner, and down at the other end of the block at Fifth and Union we still had Loveman, Berger & Teitlebaum Department Store.

That wonderful, old, crowded shopping block between Church and Union Streets had R. A. Coleman Company with electrical supplies, Model Laundry, Health Spot Shoe Shop, Cotton Shop Clothing for women, and a Hales Cut Rate Drugstore. There was a Singer Sewing Machine store, Manufacturers Outlet Shoe Store, and Morris Shop selling women's clothing.

Fifth Avenue still had our four Five & Ten Cent Stores, namely W. T. Grant Company, F. W. Woolworth, McLellan's, and S. H. Kress Company. Other stores included Feldman's Fifth Avenue Store, Allen's selling women's clothing, Foster Men's Wear, Fox Apparel, and Burt's Shoe Store.

Well, "Time Marches On." Some things change for the better, and some things change for the worse. But, the things that remain the same, constant, and endearing are our memories.

Our Aging Downtown Shopping circa 1960s

Our old downtown shopping district was aging more. What happened to all of those busy sidewalks with a sea of crowded shoppers? Even though many shoppers were living and shopping more in the beautiful suburbs of Nashville, there were still some die-hards who couldn't give up the nostalgia of the old days. The sidewalks were not overly crowded with happy shoppers, but the sidewalks were still used by some.

Remembering the 1960s, let's take one more walk down the streets of Nashville's downtown.

Let's start again at the corner of Church Street and Fifth Avenue. On the south side of Church, we are now standing in front of a beautiful department store. Cain-Sloan Company moved their store from across the street where Harvey's had elaborate plans of expansion.

Historic McKendree Methodist Church still stands on Church Street between Fifth and Sixth Avenues. Across the alley from the church stands the Tennessee Theatre aglow with its coming attractions. The Tennessee Theatre, one of the finest in the South, had art work in its inner lobby that depicted the heritage of our great state of Tennessee.

Still in this block between Fifth and Sixth, we see Inman Jewelers, Harrison Brothers Floral Company, and the same 12-story building on the corner; but, the name has evolved from the Warner Building to the Sudekum Building, and later to the Tennessee Building. And, no, the musicians' union office is not there. It has moved out to the new building the members built on Division Street. Just for fun, I looked, and the old union office was occupied by an insurance company.

On the other side of Church Street, we now have the blossoming and interesting Harvey's Department Store with its escalators, third floor Monkey Bar for children, the carousel horses and other pieces used as decorations, the real carousel which the children could ride, and the Harvey's Downstair's Dinette serving the great apple pie made by the same cook who used to make the pie at Kleeman's Restaurant.

Walking on west on Church Street, let's look at the old stores between Sixth and Seventh Avenues back in the 1960s.

On one side of Church Street do you remember Kay Jewelry Company, Barton's Clothing for women, Chesters, and Holiday's Shoes? After walking across Capitol Boulevard, we still had Castner-Knott Dry Goods Store. We didn't know it, but Castner's was really in its last days downtown.

On the other side of Church between Sixth and Seventh Avenues, we find that W. T. Grant Company had moved from Fifth Avenue to the corner of Sixth and Church. The Watkins Building and Watkins Institute were still there. We had a branch of the First American National Bank, and the Loew's Theatre building was still standing for a little while longer.

In that block we also had the First Federal Savings & Loan, Baker's Shoe Store, Evette's Wigs, Model Shoe Rebuilders, Flagg Brothers, and Harold L. Shyer Jewelry Store next to the Krystal which was still there.

That little sandwich shop next door had become the Tic-Toc Restaurant, and Candyland was still in operation at Seventh and Church.

Let's look at one more block. Between Seventh and Eighth Avenues on Church Street during the 1960s, we would find Grace's Inc., the Bennie-Dillon and the Doctor's Buildings. Wilson-Quick Drugstore was still in place. Also, we had the Nashville Surgical Supply, Handmacher Fashions, and the Tulane Parking was there. The old, nostalgic Tulane Hotel was not there. It was torn down in 1956.

On the other side of Church we saw more changes. We now had Gold-Silver and Company who was wholesale jewelers, we had the fine Mills Bookstore, and General Display Service. There was a branch of the Third National Bank, and the fine Zibart's Bookstore in that block. The old Paramount Theatre was still functioning, but reeling on its last leg. The Sears & Roebuck Company had moved out, and the National Stores was located at the corner of Eighth and Church.

———•———

In remembering our old downtown shopping areas, we can't neglect looking again at Capitol Boulevard and Fifth Avenue.

Joseph Frank & Sons still had a rear entrance on Capitol Boulevard. Our nostalgic, old Knickerbocker Theatre was gone. In its place, we had the Super X Drugstore which ran from Sixth Avenue back to Capitol Boulevard. That drugstore seemed so small, that I had to wonder, "How did the Knickerbocker Theatre fit into that space!"

You may remember in that block on Capitol, we had the Thrift Loan Company, a branch of the Commerce Union Bank, and the rear entrance to Grace's which was on Sixth Avenue.

A fine restaurant called Cross Keys had opened on Sixth Avenue, and there was a rear entrance to the restaurant on Capitol Boulevard.

An office building was still on Capitol, but it was now

called the Life & Casualty Building (not to be confused with the L & C Tower at Fourth and Church.) At the corner of Capitol and Union was still the back side of our historic Hermitage Hotel.

———◆———

To finish looking at the old shopping district during the 1960s, let's take a walk down Fifth Avenue. I don't hear that same chatter and happiness and screaming when we saw someone we knew. Was Nashville getting more sedate?

No, I think Nashvillians were moving to and shopping out in the beautiful suburbs of our great city. People still worked downtown, but the joyous days of friendly shopping were changing. Businesses were moving to areas surrounding Nashville. The Madison Square Shopping Center opened in 1956. Our first major indoor shopping mall was 100 Oaks Shopping Center which opened in 1968.

During the 1960s, at Fifth and Church where the present Sun Trust Bank Building sits, there was the Fifth Avenue Cigar Store. Next to it was the juice shop called Heckmann's California Orange Shop. The Krystal was still there on Fifth Avenue serving up those small hamburgers. Also, we had the Russell Stover Candies, Buddy Dale Hat Shop, the Cotton Shop, and Olshine Company.

Hales Cut-Rate Drugstore was there along with Dailey's Clothing, and the Ellis Shoe Company.

On that side of Fifth Avenue was the Arcade, and the City Directory did not list a drugstore by the Arcade in 1960. I wonder if it happened to be vacant for a short time?

Also, in that block was The Singer Company, Brooks-Kent Clothing Company, and Banks Clothing Company. The

City Directory did state that the corner of Fifth and Union was vacant in 1960.

Going back up to Fifth and Church on the other side of the street we had the side entrance to the great Harvey's Department Store. Also, we had Feldman's Fifth Avenue Store which sold women's clothing, Factory Outlet Store, and Allen's Women's Clothing Store.

As already mentioned, W. T. Grant Company had moved off of Fifth Avenue to the new location at Sixth and Church. However, the other three Five & Ten Cent Stores were still on Fifth Avenue. F. W. Woolworth was there, but McLellan's was listed as McCrory-McLellan-Green, and instead of Five & Ten Cent Store, which we had known from childhood, it was listed as "5 Cents to One Dollar Store." This designation was also given for S. H. Kress down the street. Fox Apparel and Burt's Shoe Store were on Fifth Avenue. But, our great old Loveman's was gone.

Recently, when I have written about S. H. Kress, the old Five & Ten Cent Store on Fifth Avenue, I have said that the five-story building was empty. Now, I learn that the building at 237 Fifth Avenue, North will sprout its wings as the Kress Lofts. The units' price range will be from $119,800 to $311,500.

I guess there is really nothing constant except change. In fact, change is almost constant.

Even though some old, nostalgic tastes have been vanishing from our Nashville palates, we have always been able to relish in new, and sometimes improved, tastes, aromas, sights, and sounds, transforming our great city into something different, but with the foundation of wonderful, nostalgic memories.

Vibrant Nashville continues...

In our haste in living,
it seems that only within a few ticks of time,
we have seen some of our past crumble,
and
Nashville has made an abrupt change of tempo.

Looking east from War Memorial Plaza, State Office Bldg.,
Cotton States Bldg., and the Andrew Jackson Hotel, c. 1948

What We Miss Today!

In the early 1970s, two downtown buildings were razed which we shall never see again. I miss the old Andrew Jackson Hotel at the corner of Sixth Avenue, North and Deaderick Street. That hotel was one of the few in Nashville which hired bands. All of the hotels had orchestras come in when certain organizations held their dinner-dances in their ballrooms and paid for the orchestras. But, the Andrew Jackson Hotel itself, just like the Hermitage Hotel, featured orchestras.

When WSM radio came on the air in 1925, one of the featured musical presentations on the inaugural broadcast was

Andrew Jackson Hotel, Elks Club at right

billed as "Beasley Smith's Andrew Jackson Hotel Orchestra." In a later period, a noon luncheon radio broadcast from the Andrew Jackson was heard with the Adrian McDowell Orchestra.

The Andrew Jackson Hotel was the home of the old Dee Jay Convention held each year in Nashville which later became the week called "Fan Fair." Then, the title "Fan Fair" became nostalgia in 2004 when the event was renamed "Country Music Association Festival."

On June 13, 1971, I saw with my own eyes the implosion of the old Andrew Jackson Hotel. The building came down in just a very few seconds. Along with the hotel, another building on Sixth Avenue, North was demolished to make way for development. The Elks' Club Lodge No. 72 also was razed to vacate that entire block.

From 1850, that old building served as a residence at fashionable 610 High Street (Sixth Avenue, North.) The Elks Club purchased the old home back in 1904. I remember the rocking chairs on the front porch and two iron elks which were placed at the steps of the entrance to the building.

However, a wonderful structure and new landmark was built in that space. Today, we enjoy the James K. Polk State Office Building and the Tennessee Performing Arts Center which we simply call T-PAC. Its new lobby premiered in 2003.

By the way, when the building first came on the scene, wasn't it called the Tennessee Center for the Performing Arts? If so, then we should call it TCPA! Oh, well, it doesn't matter.

Just think of all the Nashville hotels we miss today. No longer can we see the Andrew Jackson Hotel, but neither can we see the Maxwell House, Tulane, Duncan, Noel, Merchants (functioning as a hotel), Argonne, Allen, Anchor, Sam Davis, Utopia, Savoy, Underwood, Bismarck, and Clarkston. The old

James Robertson Hotel building on Seventh Avenue, North was built in 1929, and it still stands. But, it is not a hotel, it is rented out as apartments.

BUT, think of all of the great hotels we have today!

Just think of all of the theatres that we miss today in Nashville. No longer can we see the Tennessee, Paramount, Knickerbocker, Princess, Loew's Vendome, Crescent, Bijou, Orpheum, Alhambra, Rex, Fifth Avenue, Strand, Roxy, Woodland, Ritz, Belmont, Inglewood, Melrose, Belle Meade, Green Hills, Elite, and others I am sure which will come to your mind.

Another great building which we miss today in Nashville is Tony Sudekum's old Hippodrome on West End Avenue where today sits the Holiday Inn Select Vanderbilt across from Centennial Park. Over the years, that great old Hippodrome made money all year round.

Crescent, Tennessee and Loew's Theatres on Church Street

On Tuesday nights, Nick Gulas brought some fine entertainment in the form of big-time wrestling. We could see the Welsh Brothers, Farmer Brown, Len Rossi, Tojo Yamamoto, Jackie Fargo, and even Gorgeous George of TV fame. At ringside we enjoyed War Horse Rogers.

On weekends, the old Hippodrome may have been used as a convention center for trade shows. Political rallies were held there back in the old days. Name bands came in periodically. I got to see and hear Benny Goodman, Harry James, Elliott Lawrence, and Woody Herman, for instance.

And, other nights the Hippodrome was a grand and spacious skating rink. Oh, how I wish I could pay my 50 cents at the door, put on those skates, listen to the organ play, and get excited when the loud speaker would blast, "EVERYBODY SKATE!" Today, I could even take my grandchildren!

Opryland Becomes Nashville Nostalgia

Just a few years ago, did any of us ever think that we would be looking back at the Opryland USA Theme Park as being Nashville Nostalgia?

Opryland, which was originally developed by the National Life & Accident Insurance Company, opened in 1972. It was a 120-acre entertainment complex that offered live musical variety shows, country music concerts, children's entertainment, and thrill rides such as the Wabash Cannonball, the Flume Zoom, the Timber Topper, the Screaming Delta Demon, and other fun rides such as the Tin Lizzies, high swings which were called the Tennessee Waltz, a railroad, and the Grizzly River Rampage.

By the way, Opry Mills is now located in that area, but if you will walk to the back of Opry Mills toward the river, you can still see some of the stone forms which were a part of the Grizzly River Rampage.

The concept of Opryland USA Theme Park was inspired by the *Grand Ole Opry*. Throughout the park, the names, displays and exhibits followed the original Opry theme, and paid tribute to the greats of country music.

The park featured all types of American music. The late Paul Crabtree presented continuous entertainment in the park. Crabtree was a native Tennessean who won acclaim in New York before developing the Cumberland County Playhouse in Crossville, Tennessee. Paul's family is still building the quality of the Playhouse in Crossville. Later, George Mabry directed the musical events at the Opryland park. Today, George still teaches at Austin Peay State University and is the conductor of the Nashville Symphony Chorus.

Do you remember in 1975 that a historic Russian-American space hookup was attained when astronauts and cosmonauts rode together on Opryland's Wabash Cannonball?

Do you remember when the United Nations came to Nashville in 1976 for its first meeting outside of New York? During the visit, UN Secretary General Kurt Waldheinm and his daughter took an Opryland Flume Zoom log ride with then Tennessee Governor Ray Blanton.

My son reminded me of an outstanding theme park feature event when Opryland USA hosted a "Howl-O-Ween" weekend family celebration at the end of the 1989 season.

For that event, all Opryland guests were encouraged to bring a carved pumpkin to enter in a jack-o'-lantern show and contest. The event was held in the Nashville Network studios, and prizes were awarded.

The master-of-ceremonies for the event was WSM-TV, channel 4's, Sir Cecil Creape. You remember him as the host of the late-night television horror shows called *Creature Feature*, and *Phantom of the Opry*.

When National Life built the Opryland complex, they had more than just the theme park in mind. They looked upon the complex as including the Grand Ole Opry House which opened in 1974, and it is still with us. It is considered to be one of the finest concert venues in the country. It seats 2,000 on the floor level, and another 2,400 in the balcony. The stage is 110 feet wide and 68 feet deep.

Nashville nostalgia was brought to the new Opry House by placing in the center of its stage a 6-feet disk of dark oak flooring which was brought over from the famous Ryman

Auditorium, the former home of the *Grand Ole Opry*. When the performers play the new Opry House today, they still have a little of the old Ryman Auditorium with them.

In 1977, the Opryland Hotel opened with 600 rooms. In 1983, the hotel's Phase II expansion was completed. This phase added an additional 467 rooms along with its breathtaking Conservatory with indoor tropical gardens which featured waterfalls.

In 1988, Opryland Hotel's Phase III expansion was completed increasing room capacity to 1,891. In addition to rooms, a two-acre water Cascade area was added.

In 1991, Phase IV added convention space, the indoor Delta River on which you can ride in boats, plus more rooms. The hotel now boasts 2,879 guest rooms, 85 meeting rooms, 5 ballrooms, and a huge exhibit hall.

The General Jackson Showboat was part of the Opryland idea complex as well as the Roy Acuff Museum, the Minnie Pearl Museum, and the Grand Ole Opry Museum.

Some of these things are still with us, so the term Opryland is still used today by Gaylord Enterprises for that large area, but it doesn't include the Opryland USA Theme Park which closed at the end of the 1997 season.

Thankfully, we still have some good memories. Before the park closed, my wife and I got to take our children and then our grandchildren to the park. And, all of us got splashed and soakin' wet by riding the Grizzly River Rampage.

Life Can Be a Picnic

I guess I have been on a picnic for most of my life. If we weed-out the bad times and disappointments, and relish in the memories of what's good, then, yes, we have been on a picnic for most of our lives.

I can allow my memories to dwell on my love of music, playing at radio stations, playing in Big Bands, playing shows with internationally known artists, playing in symphony and opera orchestras, having wonderful friends, writing, composing music and hearing it performed.

Then, when I couple this with the love of working in my church, relishing in the eternal love of God, being blessed with a wonderful, loving family, and living in freedom in the greatest country in the world (God, Family, and Country), then, YES, I have been on a picnic for most of my life.

When I was a kid, my family often went to Old Jefferson Springs on the Stones River for a wonderful family picnic and outing. My sister and I played out on the water on inner tubes which Daddy took out of the tires on the car. Mother packed some of the finest picnics imaginable to eat even though it was during The Great Depression.

When we were ready to go back home, Daddy would put the inner tubes back in the tires, and we would head home.

Back in the old days, I remember all of the church picnics we attended. After church service, the kids would run to the creek, find flat rocks, and skip them on the water across the creek while the whole congregation of adults would spread food brought by every family in the church.

We are Methodists, so I guess we honestly acquired the name "Chicken Eatin' Methodists." After all of the food was laid out, there would be about six big trays of chicken cooked in about five different ways.

Sonia, my wife, has often reminisced about the great family reunions she used to attend as a child where picnics flourished.

Also, as George Peabody College students, my wife and I didn't let a picnic get by us there either. Every Fourth of July, the beautiful Peabody campus would be a mass of tables on which would be hundreds of watermelons. The college faculty, wearing appropriate white aprons, cut and served ice-cold watermelon slices to everyone. The large waste baskets by the tables held enough watermelon rinds to bring the Cumberland River to flood-stage.

After my wife and I got married and had children, we found picnics the way of life. Often we would go to Centennial Park or Shelby Park with a big basket of food. The kids would enjoy feeding the ducks. Then, we as a family sat at a picnic table and ate our bounty which formed nostalgic memories for a lifetime.

As our kids grew, we enjoyed cooking out in our backyard. I am reminded of a time when I must have been feeling especially hospitable and I invited several other families in the neighborhood to come over and eat. I thought I had enough food!!

Everyone began to eat and I continued to cook. You can't imagine how some of those kids inhaled enormous portions of food. I began to run out of things to cook. I gave out with a yell of distress and emergency. Then, neighbors began running to their homes and bringing in more food. I kept on cooking.

It was fun, and everybody did get a fair share of the picnic. I told my wife, the next time I think I have enough food, let's double the order!

More recently, we have had picnics with our children and our five grandchildren. Now, at my age, I can let some of the others plan the menu, cook the food, serve the food, and allow me to sit there in the beauty of our Tennessee hills, and soak in all of the wonderful sights and memories of days gone by. I think human beings are at their best when they are in contact with God's nature.

We live in the beautiful community of Bellevue in the suburbs of Nashville. We have an annual Bellevue Picnic in the Red Caboose Park each Spring. The Bellevue Chamber of Commerce offers booths of business, crafts, church, and civic interests. There is entertainment, music, rides for the children, and a spectacular fireworks display at the end of the evening.

After reading this, you might think that my whole life has been just one big picnic. While allowing my nostalgic spirit and memories to take over, I think you just might be right. Life has been one BIG PICNIC!

Times, People, Places and Things

A variety of memories—
A smorgasbord of Nashville's nostalgic tastes

Formal reception for opening of the Tennessee Theatre

Times, People, Places and Things

There used to be an alley downtown running between Union Street and Church Street. The alley ran parallel to Sixth and Seventh Avenues. Around the turn of the 20th century, the government widened Union Street, widened Eighth Avenue, and converted that alley into a working road that we know today as Capitol Boulevard.

Just north of our Tennessee State Capitol building, a community was established in the 1850s by German immigrants. Germantown was the first suburb in North Nashville. The citizens of Germantown celebrate each year their Oktoberfest.

Among many interesting things to see in Germantown are two churches. The attractive Monroe Street United Methodist Church is at one corner of Seventh Avenue and Monroe Street. On another corner of Seventh and Monroe is the Assumption Church which is the second oldest Catholic church in Nashville, dedicated in 1859.

This old Assumption Church in Germantown even had sermons spoken in German until World War I. Of course, the oldest Catholic church in Nashville is Saint Mary's Church on Fifth Avenue, North downtown.

Do you remember the two sets of streetcar tracks running on Church Street back in the old days? Streetcars ran east on one track and west on the other. During my youth over the years, a streetcar would run on Church Street passing such stores as Castner- Knott, Lebeck Brothers, Chandler's Shoes, Warner Drugstore, Cain-Sloan Company, the Watkins Institute Building, Joy Floral Company, Flagg Brothers Shoes, Sam Small Jewelry, Lerner Shop, the Jackson Building, Candy's Inc., White Trunk and Bag Company, Kay Jewelers, the Paramount, Loew's and Princess Theatres, Fred Goldner Jewelers located next door to Loew's Theatre, and a shop which was called Tick Tock Frox.

———— • ————

Francis Craig, songwriter of "Near You," "Beg Your Pardon," and "Red Rose" among others, had a wonderful orchestra that played NBC radio programs from the old Studio C at radio station WSM. His orchestra played for 21 consecutive years at the Grill Room of the Hermitage Hotel. Also, he played around the country for many engagements. He was well-known throughout the entire region.

In addition to many fine musicians and vocalists over the years, Francis featured a three-feet-nine-inches tall African-American midget known simply by the name of Pee Wee. Back from the mid-thirties, Pee Wee was a singer and fine entertainer. He dressed as a hotel bellhop like Phillip Morris's "Johnny." You remember radio's Johnny who yelled, "Call—ing Phillip Mor—ris!" Nashville loved Pee Wee and invited him to entertain at many birthday parties around town.

Pee Wee's last name was Marquette. Some of you may wonder whatever happened to this dynamic personality. Well, when Pee Wee left Nashville and the Craig Orchestra, he went to New York City where he became the master-of-ceremonies at both Club Zanzibar and the great jazz location on Broadway called Birdland.

Recently, I enjoyed reading the biography of jazz musician Stan Getz. Pee Wee's name is mentioned in the book several times. Pee Wee loved Stan's playing and at Birdland introduced Stan as "one of the foremost tenor men of all time." Yes, that is the same Pee Wee (except much older) that struck my nostalgic spirit and carried me back to the Nashville forties.

———————•———————

Recently, my wife and I were invited for dinner at Mario's. If you recall, Mario started his restaurant first in a house on West End Avenue. Later, he moved on West End to an office building where he had his restaurant downstairs. Today, Mario's is located at 2005 Broadway in a beautiful, old house which is exquisite.

There were six of us at our table. As we sat there, it seemed that every word out of anyone's mouth was on the subject of nostalgia. I sat there amazed. We talked about various schools and old buildings. One gentleman talked about the first Shoney's restaurant in town which was in Madison. He mentioned the large canopy under which cars could drive up and have their food orders brought out to them.

One gentleman who was originally from Pennsylvania talked of his stay in Nashville during World War II. He was stationed at the Army Air Corps Classification Center on Thompson Lane. That old Army Center determined whether one would be a pilot, navigator, or bombardier in the Army Air Corps.

This gentleman began talking about when his whole outfit would march from Thompson Lane to old Cascade Plunge swimming pool back in 1943. At the pool he remembered a young lady who would climb to the top of a 60 or 70-feet diving tower, and dive off. He seemed to be really smitten by that young lady. He said he never dated her, but he painted her name on the front of his airplane when he began to fly missions in World War II.

He concluded his story by saying that at the end of the war, he came back to Nashville and married another girl. And, it was she and this old Army Vet who were seated at our table that evening at Mario's.

The old Nashville Vols minor league baseball team played the last game at old Sulphur Dell just north of our State Capitol in 1963.

I am sure you remember when Larry Schmittou brought minor league baseball back to Nashville. The Nashville Sounds played their first season in 1978. That year a total of 380,000 fans enjoyed good baseball at Greer Stadium.

Greer Stadium was named for Herschel Greer who was the president of the old Nashville Vols baseball team.

During the 1960s, Civil Rights of all citizens was a topic in which grievances against segregation came to the surface. The first serious clash occurred in February of 1960 when African-American college students took seats at the lunch counters of three downtown chain stores.

Many of Nashville's citizens, including politicians, educators, and ministers began to seek corrections. Nashville was one of the first cities to advance solutions, and Nashville was considered one of the leaders in the Civil Rights movement.

Special mention with regard to civil rights achievements

should be given to Mayor Ben West, a college student at the American Baptist Theological Seminary by the name of John Lewis who is now a United States Congressman, Z. Alexander Looby who was elected as a City Councilman, and The Reverend Kelly Miller Smith who was the pastor at the First Baptist Church, Capitol Hill, among others.

When we think of good bookstores of the "Athens of the South," we have to mention the names of Zibart's and Mills.

I am pleased that our new Nashville Public Library, which had its grand opening on June 9, 2001, designated a space called Schweid-Mills Writer's Room. The room was dedicated in honor of Adele Mills Schweid and her husband, Bernie Schweid, who together ran Mills Bookstore that closed in 1990. Also honored was Adele's father, Reuben Mills, who started the business in 1892.

One of the first comic strips to appear in daily newspapers was the mischievous Katzenjammer Kids. As a child, I really enjoyed reading that strip in the "funny paper."

Other early comics were The Gumps, Mutt and Jeff, Felix the Kat, Bringing Up Father (which I called Maggie and Jiggs,) Moon Mullins, Tillie the Toiler, Gasoline Alley, and Joe Palooka.

Joe Palooka, the popular sports comic boxer, was created by Ham Fisher and first appeared in 1930. I hope you remember Joe along with his boxing manager, Knobby Walsh. And, I hope you remember the pretty, blond society girl who played the role of Joe's sweetheart. Her name was Ann Howe.

When I directed the marching band at Evansville College back in the 1960s, a French horn player in the band was named Ann Howe. You can imagine the fun we had with that name and all of the Palooka jokes. Ann was a great sport, too.

I read that there really is a "Gasoline Alley." It is Superior Street in Tomah, Wisconsin, the hometown of Frank King, who was the creator of Gasoline Alley in the comics. The city celebrates "Gasoline Alley Days" every September in remembrance of Frank King who is buried there.

<hr />

As a Boy Scout back in the late 1930s and early 1940s, I used to usher at all of the Vanderbilt home football games. Do some of you remember Louisiana's Huey Long, "The Kingfish," came to Nashville on a chartered train which he called his "Football Special," bringing the L. S. U. Band and thousands of L. S. U. supporters for the Vanderbilt-L. S. U. game?

<hr />

My wife, Sonia, and I while having dinner with Mary and Ken Berryhill, "The world's oldest living disc jockey," had great fun remembering old Nashville radio announcers from the nostalgic days of radio before television took over. Ken and I even continued our conversation later talking about some great radio broadcasters in Nashville. Ken Berryhill himself was an announcer at the old WMAK when the station was located on the lower floor of the old Maxwell House Hotel.

Ken Berryhill is still going strong. He broadcasts his award winning radio program called *The Old Record Shop* as well as country shows over station WRVU radio, 91.1 FM. *The Old Record Shop* also airs over radio station WAMB, 1160 AM. In addition, he produces shows over radio WNQM from Nashville, and the shows are sent out short-wave radio heard around the world.

In our conversations, we mentioned Ken Bramming at WSM-FM and WAMB, and Bill "Hoss" Allen at WLAC. Ken Berryhill mentioned Noel Ball. He mentioned Joe Nixon who was at WMAK in the old days. But then, both of us shouted out the name of Joe Allison.

I remember when I listened to Joe Allison every morning. Joe had a great program of spinning pop tunes of the day. The greatness was not just the music with his program, it was Joe. His chatters were as great as his platters. Then Ken said, "I have Joe's phone number. Why don't you call him?" So, I did.

It was a thrill to hear that voice that I had enjoyed so many years before. Joe Allison also was on *Noontime Neighbors* at WSM radio with John McDonald. How many of you remember that name?

In my conversation with Joe, he mentioned some names that brought a nostalgic spirit to my soul. At old WKDA radio, he mentioned Hugh Cherry. Then, I remembered Larry Munson. Larry is still at WSB in Atlanta. Joe reminded me that Ralph Emery was at WSIX as well as announcer Al Martin. And, Joe mentioned Jerry Thomas who was at WMAK as well as WSM-FM. Jerry was the first announcer for WSM-FM.

Then, I remembered that Otto Bash was at WSM and WSIX. I and Otto, a fine drummer, have played a million band jobs together over the years. The next time I had a conversation with Otto, he reminded me of Jim Kent back in the old days who was a fine announcer and the program director at

WSIX. Otto also mentioned Joe Calloway, Charlie Scott, and Jack Simpson at WSIX.

Sorrowfully, Joe Allison passed away shortly after I talked with him on the phone in 2002. I am so thankful that we talked, I gave him a few things to remember, and both of us were nostalgically lifted with a delightful conversation of old memories.

———•———

I remember Larry Munson well. I first heard him on radio station WKDA back in the 1940s when he was a disc-jockey playing great music by the Big Bands. When Larry came to Nashville, he announced high school ball games and the old Nashville Vols baseball games.

Then, the station manager wanted him to do Vanderbilt basketball games. In 1947, Larry announced the first Vandy game at the old Father Ryan High School gym when the school was on Elliston Place. Munson also announced Vanderbilt football, and for 23 years he was host of a popular TV fishing show in Nashville.

Larry Munson moved to Atlanta in 1966 to call the Atlanta Braves games. Then, he began calling the University of Georgia football that same year and hasn't missed a season since.

———•———

Do you remember the old Granny White Market located near Radnor Lake at the corner of Otter Creek Road and Granny White Pike? That store began operation in 1927. In 1987, the store was owned by Reese Smith, Jr. and was operated by Helen and Howard Maxon.

All of us remember when we had the opportunity to read editorials of different points of view in *The Tennessean* and the *Nashville Banner*. In spite of this editorial difference, publisher James G. Stahlman of the *Nashville Banner*, and Silliman Evans of *The Tennessean* signed a contract in 1937 whereby they would pool the business operations of the two newspapers, such as circulation, advertising, accounting, and printing. They formed this Newspaper Printing Corporation which remained in tact until the closing of the *Nashville Banner* in 1998.

Many of you Big Band buffs will remember the great Jimmie Lunceford band. Jimmie graduated from Fisk University with a Bachelor of Music degree. The Jimmie Lunceford Orchestra was nationally famous. The band recorded such hits as "Margie," "My Blue Heaven," "Ain't She Sweet?" and "Blues in the Night."

Do you remember those wonderful, colorful, inexpensive ten-cent pulps? You probably remember *The Shadow*, *The Spider*, *Nick Carter*, and *Doc Savage*.

Did you ever save those S & H Green Stamps? Years ago, my wife and I got several items for our home by turning in those green stamps for lamps, kitchen items, towels, and the like.

Today, teenagers might go to a fast-food restaurant to get

hired. Back when I was a teenager, we tried to get jobs as a soda jerk, a movie theatre usher, or an elevator operator.

I used to be able to jerk a pretty good chocolate soda. I would take one of those tall soda glasses, throw it up in the air, and catch it after one turn. Then, I put some chocolate syrup in the glass, squirted a fierce stream of carbonated water in the glass to whirl the syrup around, squirt more carbonated water, and then put in a good scoop of vanilla ice cream. I would top it off with some whipped cream and a cherry. Then, when friends drank it with a straw, they sucked all of it up and played what we called the "Drugstore Blues."

Movie theatres needed ushers carrying flashlights to escort the patrons to seats in the dark theatre. The movies never stopped. We could enter the theatre at anytime we wanted, and stay as long as we wanted.

Back in my youth, the self-service elevators had not been invented, or at least were not used in office buildings and department stores. An operator stood in the elevator and turned the handle to close the door and have the elevator go up or down.

In office buildings, the operator would call out the floor numbers. It was more fun in the department stores, because the elevator operator had a definite spiel to yell out, such as: "Second floor... children's apparel... Third floor... home appliances... Fourth floor... ladies read-to-wear, hats, brassieres, corsets, high-heel shoes, and please watch your step!"

———— • ————

You may have known Katharen Tate and her sister who were fine dancers who performed all around Nashville. They became professional dancers and traveled all over the country in stage presentations. Katharen and her sister performed on one of the first Camel Caravans to entertain the troops during World War II.

Their father was a streetcar motorman, and later a bus driver. Their good friend was Adelaide Hendricks Hazelwood. Her father was a streetcar motorman, also. Adelaide later took on the professional name of Del Wood who played on the *Grand Ole Opry* and recorded on Music Row.

There is something else interesting about Katharen Tate with Nashville ties. One time after church, Katharen and her boyfriend were having a treat at Candyland at the corner of Seventh Avenue and Church Street, and her boyfriend, Leslie, proposed to her. It was during World War II when Leslie was stationed at the Army Air Corps Classification Center off of Thompson Lane where he had been classified as a bombardier. Katharen said that they originally met at the "Cadet Room" in the old Noel Hotel where she was a volunteer. Sadly, Leslie was killed in a raid over Germany, but Katharen said that she kept in touch with Leslie's mother and an aunt until they were gone.

----◆----

When I met my wife, Sonia Anne Young, McKendree Methodist Church, located downtown on Church Street between Fifth and Sixth Avenues, was her family's church. So, I became familiar with the church, the choir, the ministers, and the activities of the great church.

The church was named in honor of William McKendree who was the first American-born bishop of the Methodist denomination. He visited Nashville as early as 1797, and he was present for the dedication of the first Methodist church building in 1833.

Several inaugural ceremonies for numerous governors of our state were held at McKendree Church including Andrew Johnson, Neill S. Brown, Aaron V. Brown, and William B. Campbell. Also, the funeral service for President James K. Polk was conducted there with the Reverend John Berry McFerrin officiating.

Back in the old days, Spring Street had so many churches on, near, or around it that the street's name was changed from Spring Street to Church Street.

Even in my lifetime, I can remember the Vine Street Christian Church, and the Vine Street Temple located in that area. Before the 1900s and later, many of the churches moved to the suburbs because that was where their members were moving.

Today, only four churches remain on or near Church Street: the three that were there first, McKendree Methodist Church, built in 1910; the historic First Presbyterian Church, which is now the Downtown Presbyterian Church at the corner of Fifth and Church, dedicated on Easter Sunday, 1851; and, Saint Mary's Cathedral on Fifth Avenue. Richard Pius Miles, first Roman Catholic bishop of Nashville, officiated at the laying of the cornerstone of St. Mary's on June 6, 1845. The fourth church is the Central Church of Christ, which is located on Fifth Avenue just off of Church Street.

———◆———

We remember the Cheek family's success with its Maxwell House Coffee being named for the old Maxwell House Hotel at Fourth and Church, and having President Theodore Roosevelt initiating the long-standing slogan by saying the coffee was "Good to the last drop."

But, did you know that "Fit for a King Coffee," which was prepared by the H. G. Hill Company of Nashville, was accounted to have been a factor in Hill's success?

———•———

Do you remember the name of Gene Autry's horse? When I was a kid, the old Paramount Theatre on Church Street advertised that a Saturday show would present Gene Autry and his horse, Champion, on stage. I went to the theatre, waited a long time in line, and then got into a seat to see only Champion. Because of some problem, probably because of a union restriction, Gene Autry could not appear on stage. Oh well, it was terrific to get to see Champion.

In the old Western movies, just as the crooks were about to escape, Gene would say, "Boys, let's go head 'em off at the pass. But, before we go, I want to sing you a little song."

Do you realize that he never wanted to sing a big song! It was always, "I want to sing you a little song." Those great Westerns and songs brought joy to our lives.

———•———

Do you remember when there used to be a drive up to the State Capitol at the side of the building? It was used for a hundred years. In the 1950s, the road was removed, and cars were made to approach the State Capitol building from the rear.

I am sure you have seen the chief monument on the State Capitol grounds which is an equestrian statue of General Andrew Jackson. There are only two other castings of this statue in existence. One is in Lafayette Square in Washington, D.

C., and the other is in Jackson Square in New Orleans, Louisiana.

———•———

Do you remember the Rudy Farm in Pennington Bend near Opryland with its herd of real live buffalo?

Did your mother ever collect Jewel Tea dishes? Those custard cups were especially nice. I can remember that old Jewel Tea truck driving up in front of our house every now and then.

When I was a child, my family banked at the First American National Bank which was located downtown at the corner of Fourth Avenue and Union Street. Its final resting place before merging or being sold was the new Nashville City Center on Union Street near the Public Square. The Cumberland Club of Nashville was located on the 26th floor where once I got to see the sights of Nashville while playing a dinner-dance for the Newspaper Printing Corporation from that high vantage point.

The Cumberland Club opened to downtown members in 1947 on the second floor of the old Maxwell House Hotel. The club relocated to the Nashville City Center in 1989. Sorrowfully, the club closed in August of 2004.

———•———

In the 1940s, after I returned from the Army of World War II, I played many dance jobs with various bands at the old Army Air Corps base in Smyrna, Tennessee. I understand that it was the first big bomber school in the United States.

I played in bands at the Non-Coms (Non-commissioned

officers) Club, but mainly at the fine Officer's Club. They had a beautiful club, and expected the very best in music.

In March of 1950, as part of a nation-wide Air Force commemoration, the old Smyrna Air Field was dedicated as Sewart Air Force Base, in honor of Major Allan J. Sewart, Jr. Major Sewart was at Pearl Harbor at the time of the Japanese attack. He saw fighting in the battle of Midway, and was killed in action in the Solomon Islands in 1942. Major Sewart had attended Hume-Fogg High School.

———•———

Communities today make donations to charities through the United Way. Do you remember when the community program of giving was called U. G. F.? It stood for United Givers Fund. And, I can remember even before that when the community project was called the Community Chest.

Have you ever visited our Nashville Children's Theatre? It is located off of Second Avenue, South near Rutledge Hill. It is at the north end of the old, fort-like building which used to be a building in the old University of Nashville.

The Nashville's Children's Theatre is a nonprofit, professional, Actors' Equity theatre which was founded in 1931 by the Junior League of Nashville, and is the oldest children's theatre in the country. Our children, and now our grandchildren are enjoying some very fine theatre there.

———•———

Vanderbilt University plays a large role in keeping up the public's awareness of astronomy. There is an observatory on the Vanderbilt campus which the public may visit at night at no charge. And, the A. J. Dyer Observatory on Oman Drive off of Granny White Pike has a public night each month, free to visitors.

Through Vanderbilt and members of the Barnard-Seyfert Astronomical Society, they update folks on what is happening on the local scene through lectures, and "starry" night events.

Many of you will remember Dr. Carl Seyfert, a professor at Vanderbilt, who was the first weatherman at WSM-TV, channel 4, back in the 1950s. He was an excellent weatherman, and he livened up his reports by throwing in astronomical tidbits.

Dr. Seyfert was responsible for the building of the Dyer Observatory, and was its director in the late 1950s. All of us were saddened when he was killed in an automobile accident in 1960.

Other weather men at channel 4 over the years included Boyce Hawkins, and the famous *Wheel of Fortune* television star Pat Sajak. Bill Williams was given the title of "The Rhyming Weatherman." Also, back when the weather people used a board and chalk, George Goldtrap used the gimmick of throwing the chalk up in the air and catching it in his coat pocket.

When WSM-TV, channel 4, came on the scene, it is no wonder that it gave Nashvillians the image of being a station of high quality because of such outstanding people involved, such as Dr. Carl Seyfert, Jack DeWitt, Elmer Alley, Marjorie Cooney, Francis Craig, Beasley Smith, Owen Bradley, many fine announcers, and live musicians, among others.

———◆———

One of the oldest poster-making companies in the country still operates in Nashville. The place is located at 316

Broadway. The company was founded by C. R. and H. H. Hatch in 1879. In the 1920s, Will T. Hatch hand-carved the wood blocks used in the printing press process. I guess many country music fans have at least one Hatch Showprint.

I understand that 3111 Hydes Ferry Pike which was owned by Jeff Hyde is still standing. It is reported that both Jesse James and his brother Frank James with their families lived in that house for about a year around 1879.

Can you remember the chewing gum counters which contained gums of many different flavors including Blackjack, Clove, and Teaberry?

Do you remember when laundry detergents had free glasses, dishes, or towels hidden inside the box?

Do you remember when your mother and grandmother used hatpins? They wouldn't go anywhere without the proper headwear to match their outfit. And, they secured their hats with an heirloom hatpin.

Do you remember when a photographer would come around the neighborhoods with a pony? You could have your child's photo made while he or she sat on the pony.

Do you remember when television came into our homes in the 1950s? Also, that created the invention of the TV dinners. I guess that was the beginning of our downfall. That was the end of family dinner conversations. Family members sat with a TV tray, ate a TV dinner, and watched TV!

How many of you have ever stood at the top of the steps

to the entrance of Percy Warner Park which overlooks Belle Meade Boulevard? In days gone by, you may have looked down at that scene from horseback while enjoying the well-kept bridle paths through the park.

This entrance to the park was a project built by the WPA (Works Progress Administration) back during the New Deal of President Franklin D. Roosevelt. The park used to have a horse stable, a riding academy, and you could reserve a horse to take over the nice bridle paths through the park for a very nominal fee.

The Nashville Electric Service building on Church Street was built in 1952. The large dome on top of the building contained a revolving multi-colored beacon searchlight. Do you remember when that light was turned on at night? Years ago when we realized that energy was a thing to conserve, the revolving beacon light was no longer turned on at night.

When we used to have Five & Ten Cent Stores, do you remember how we could pop a balloon at the soda fountain to see what the price of our banana split would cost?

Did you know that Cameron Middle School over on First Avenue in South Nashville used to be a high school? It was Cameron High School from 1957 to 1971. The Cameron Alumni Association made plans to create a Cameron Archives Room at the present Cameron Middle School.

Do you remember the old Berry Field airport where we had to go outdoors to get on the plane? It was also built with

WPA funds during the nation's recovery from The Great Depression.

Nashville's Berry Field was served first by American Airlines and then by Eastern Airlines after the airport was opened in 1936.

The WPA was administered in Tennessee by Colonel Harry S. Berry, and when Nashville got the airport through this program, it was named Berry Field in honor of Colonel Berry.

Even today at our International Airport, you will see the letters BNA on our luggage which stands for Nashville. The B in those letters stands for Berry.

<hr>

When we were kids, we had our share of silly songs. I hope you remember "Three Little Fishes in An It-i-bitty pool," "Ain't Nobody Here but Us Chickens," "Hey Ba-Ba Re-Bop," "Aba Daba Honeymoon," "Open the Door, Richard," "Chickery Chick," "Cement Mixer Putty Putty," "Milkman, Keep Those Bottles Quiet," "Flat Foot Floogie with a Floy Floy," and "Mairzy Doats."

The real lyrics to "Mairzy Doats" when spoken slowly are: "Mares eat oats, and does eat oats, and little lambs eat ivy." Now, say the line real fast...

<hr>

Do you remember the old ferry off of Charlotte Pike which took you and your car across the Cumberland River? Also, there was a ferry in Inglewood which crossed the river close to where Opry Mills is today. The ferries were free, because the State Department of Transportation felt that using the ferries were more inexpensive than having to build bridges. Of course, today we have many bridges in Nashville. Those old ferries bring back some fun memories though.

———•———

When I was a child, my mother's cure for a sore throat and cough was to have me wear a flannel cloth tightly around my neck covered with Vick salve when I went to bed. I hated it! Even today, I cannot stand flannel against my skin. But, it seems like the treatment must have worked.

In my reading, I have been intrigued to learn what the pioneers who settled Nashville used for various sicknesses and treatment. They used bear grease to remove corns and bunions. Rattlesnake grease eased rheumatic pains. A wild-onion poultice helped a stiff neck. An extract from the bark of the Dogwood flowering tree was used by Native Americans and later by early settlers in Tennessee to treat fevers.

One thing that I did like as a child was a cup of sassafras tea. It was made by boiling the root of the red sassafras. It was good!

———•———

Our first major indoor, suburban shopping mall was One Hundred Oaks which opened in 1968. I can remember the land at that location on Thompson Lane before the mall was built. A fine home sat on the land which was called One Hundred Oaks. Sadly, by the time of the mall opening, most of us had said "Good bye" to downtown shopping.

Do you remember the fun we used to have with the old style pop bottle tops? The inside of each bottle cap contained a cork disk which assured a good seal on the bottle. We would take our pocket knives and carefully pop out this cork. Then, we could place the bottle cap on our shirt by pushing the cork disk through from the other side to hold the cap on our shirt. The bottle top clung as if by magic.

So, we proudly walked around displaying our Coca-Cola, Pepsi Cola, Royal Crown Cola, and Nehi bottle caps. Nehi drinks were especially good because of the flavors and the colors of caps. We had an orange cap off of a big orange drink bottle, and purple from a grape drink. An Orange Crush bottle cap showed up well, too.

In 1865, Dr. William E. Ward opened Ward's Seminary for young ladies in Nashville. The buildings were at the corner of old Summer Street (Fifth Avenue, North) and Cedar Street (Charlotte Avenue.) Later, the school moved into new buildings erected on old Spruce Street (Eighth Avenue, North) between Church and Broad Streets next to the Savage House, an old townhouse of early Nashville, which is still present today at 167 Eighth Avenue.

Joseph Acklen had been dead a number of years when in 1889, Adelicia Acklen died in Washington, D. C., and Acklen Hall at Belmont was sold to two ladies by the names of Miss Ida Hood and Miss Susan Heron. These two ladies opened the first Belmont College.

As the story goes, these two ladies began to feel the wear and tear of running the school. So, in 1912, after 22 years of having the college serve the students, they sold Belmont to a purchasing corporation which also had bought Ward's Seminary.

On June 1, 1913, Ward's Seminary and Belmont College merged and chartered Ward-Belmont School. This became one of the finest girls' finishing schools in the country.

The great old school closed in 1951 after having taught such famous personalities as our Opry's Minnie Pearl, and Broadway actress Mary Martin. It seems that the school was more ambitious than the enrollment justified after they erected some costly buildings. The banks foreclosed, and the Southern Baptist Convention bought the property. Thus, another college using the same name as the old Belmont College opened in September of 1951.

There was a group of Nashvillians which didn't want to see the fine preparatory training for young ladies disappear from Nashville. So, they insisted that a faculty member at Ward-Belmont by the name of Mrs. Susan Souby would be the principal of a new private school for girls.

Mrs. Souby had been the director of the high school department at old Ward-Belmont. At the time of the closing of Ward-Belmont, she was negotiating to accept a position at George Peabody College for Teachers.

However, wanting to see a fine preparatory school for girls continue in Nashville, she became the school principal of the new established Harpeth Hall School which still maintains the excellent standards set by its predecessor. The school is located on Hobbs Road. It has grown, and is still growing into a beautiful campus.

Do you remember when a hotel was built at the corner of Seventh Avenue, North and Union Street? That is where the old Y. M. C. A. building sat for many years. In addition to the

Y. M. C. A., the old eight-story building housed the Nashville Business College, and the YMCA School of Law.

The hotel built at that location has gone under several different names. Today, it is the Sheraton Hotel. When the new hotel was first built there, it was the Hyatt Regency Hotel with the revolving Polaris Restaurant on top. We ate there many times and looked out over the Nashville skyline as the restaurant slowly turned around.

The first time we were there, we walked around enjoying looking at the new restaurant. As we were having trouble finding the way back to our table, I said to my wife, "You can get turned around up here."

O. K. Where is the drum crash?

———————•———————

For you who think that happenings are not in an overall plan for our lives, then dwell on this story. A man by the name of Hill Carlen who lives in Cookeville, Tennessee was driving through Bellevue one day, he happened to stop his car for some reason, and saw a stack of *Westview* Newspapers on a rack. He opened a copy of the paper, saw the column called "Nashville Nostalgia," and began to read.

My column for that issue had to do with the Old City Cemetery, and in the column I mentioned my father-in-law, Mr. T. C. Young, who after retiring from the coal business was asked by Mayor Ben West to manage the Old City Cemetery.

This Mr. Carlen from Cookeville is very interested in genealogy, and is seriously tracing the Moore family tree of which he is a part. When he read the name T. C. Young in the *Westview*, it occurred to him that his father had visited with this Mr. Young in Nashville. He knew that Mr. Young had married an Adaline Moore. So, Mr. Carlen went to the telephone, looked up my name in the phone book as the writer of the column which he had seen, and placed his call.

My wife, Sonia, answered the phone. Sonia is a member of that Moore family into which T. C. Young had married. So, these two Moore descendants who didn't know each other talked for about an hour on the phone.

*T.C. Young
at Old City Cemetery*

Then, one day Mr. Carlen asked to come to our home as he could show Sonia many wonderful pictures and relate much information about the Moore family which was a great interest to Sonia. The day Mr. Carlen came happened to be a day that our daughter, Lee Anne Thompson Parsley, and our oldest granddaughter, Katy Parsley, were visiting with us.

The meeting was wonderful as we discussed the ancestral facts of the Moore family, and looked at pictures from both Mr. Carlen's collection and ones that Sonia had stashed away, while we munched on Sonia's wonderful cookies and tea.

The moral of the story is that it created interest within Sonia, our daughter, and our granddaughter to become more aware of tracing the family's history, and gaining a wealth of information that should be passed on to future generations. Mr. Carlen's research revealed that the Moore family tree is made up of good stock, has produced many servants of the Lord, and a family in which all can be proud.

All of that "happened" because that day Mr. Carlen "happened" to drive through Bellevue, "happened" to stop his car, "happened" to see a stack of *Westview* Newspapers, "happened" to open to the page on which "Nashville Nostalgia" mentioned Mr. T. C. Young, and thereby made his phone call!

———•———

Did you ever wonder why apples float? An apple is made up of 25% air. That is why apples float on water, and we can bob for apples on Halloween! We have heard all of our lives that "an apple a day keeps the doctor away."

Medical education has always been important in Nashville. In addition to the medical departments of the old University of Nashville, Vanderbilt University, and Central Tennessee College (which today is Meharry Medical School), we also had Shelby Medical College, and Nashville Medical College. In time, Shelby and Vanderbilt merged. Vanderbilt and Meharry remain with us today to carry on the tradition of medical education in Nashville.

———•———

Do you recall the beginnings of stardom for Nashville's Pat Boone? At age 16, Pat hosted a radio show called *Youth on Parade* at WSIX radio. Pat sang all around town and on radio and television. He later married Shirley Foley, the daughter of country music star Red Foley. Then, after winning on *Arthur Godfrey's Talent Scouts,* Pat went on to fame as a recording artist and even into the movies.

Do you remember when we first had to buy that "green sticker" which we had to apply to our automobile windshield to indicate payment of a wheel or "use" tax?

Flat Rock is the name that early settlers to Nashville gave the area that now is called Woodbine. Back in 1939, Flat Rock was officially renamed Woodbine.

From the early 1900s to 1941, the old streetcars operated by the Nashville Railway and Light Company provided transportation between downtown Nashville and the Radnor community which is just south of Woodbine.

In the late 1880s, there was a spring at the corner of Nolensville Road and Thompson Lane where citizens watered their horses. At that location today sits a White Castle restaurant.

Back when I was a child, I never missed hearing *Little Orphan Annie* on the radio. The program was sponsored by Ovaltine. I loved that program. Also, I loved Ovaltine. At the end of the program on occasions, special offers were made for which you could write in and receive through the mail.

I remember when the announcer said that we could write in for a Little Orphan Annie code ring. Codes would be given over the air, and we could decode the messages with our Little Orphan Annie code ring.

Naturally, being an avid Ovaltine drinker, I collected my labels and mailed them off for my code ring. Sure enough, one day, Mr. Fuller, our postman, delivered the special offer to my home mailbox on the front porch.

At the end of the next radio program when a code was announced, I meticulously wrote down each number so I could decode the message. It was a simple code. It was certainly no code which the Germans or Japanese could not have broken during World War II.

That first code which I decoded with my Little Orphan Annie code ring following that broadcast spelled out the exciting code, "Drink more Ovaltine!"

————•————

Back in the late 1940s when I had a class with Dr. Alfred Leland Crabb at George Peabody College, I can remember how much he talked about the great value of Nashville's Watkins Institute.

The school was named for Samuel Watkins, a noted brick manufacturer and builder in Nashville. Also, Watkins served under General Andrew Jackson at the Battle of New Orleans. At Watkins' death in 1880, he gave the property located at Sixth Avenue and Church Street plus $100,000 as an endowment for a school later called Watkins Institute.

This school was a pioneer school for adult education, and it has been in continuous operation in Nashville since 1885. I remember that John A. Hood was the school director for many years when I was coming up.

Watkins Institute remained at the corner of Sixth Avenue and Church Street for many years. The school had to vacate when the new Nashville Public Library was built. Still going strong, Watkins for a time was located at 100 Powell Place in South Nashville. Later, the school moved into the old vacant Fountain Square movie multiplex in Metro-Center north of

Nashville. And, the name of the school is now Watkins College of Art Design.

———————•·•——————

When I used to play with some of the old-time Nashville musicians in the American Legion Band after World War II, I heard them speak of a band leader by the name of Tony Rose.

Tony was a Nashville musician, band leader, and city councilman who lived from 1879 until 1940. In 1940, the city named a park called "Rose Park" in his honor. You may remember that the lot at the corner of 16th Avenue, South and Division Street where the old Country Music Hall of Fame building stands was once this Tony Rose Park.

———————•·•——————

The YMHA (Young Men's Hebrew Association) and the YWHA (Young Women's Hebrew Association) used to be located on Union Street between Seventh and Eighth Avenues, North next to the old National Life & Accident Insurance Company building which was located at the corner of Seventh and Union.

When I first joined the Nashville Symphony Orchestra, I recall that we held some of the rehearsals in the old YMHA building. There were bronze plaques located at the entrance of the old YMHA and YWHA on Union Street stating when they were organized, when the building was erected and the names of the officers. Today, those plaques are located in the Jewish Community Center.

———•———

When television came upon the scene in Nashville, movie theatres began to suffer for lack of an audience. The theatres tried everything to rebuild their audiences. Sometimes the theatres gave away free dishes. Also, do you remember when the theatres would hold Bank Night? Merchandise was donated by local businesses, and a drawing was held during the showing of the movies to see who the winners would be that night.

I hope you remember our old Carnegie Library built in 1904 at Eighth and Union. The building was razed around the year 1965. Later, the Ben West Library was built on that site.

Did you know that the fountain and court area of our new Nashville Public Library on Church Street displays a replica of the front of our old Carnegie Library? It is worth seeing and holding our memories of the old library.

You realize that there are still two Carnegie libraries in Nashville built with funds from philanthropist Andrew Carnegie. They are the North Branch Carnegie and the East Branch Carnegie libraries.

———•———

I wonder if you know the first name given to the high school built in 1938 from which I graduated at the big corner of West End and Bowling Avenues. While the school was being built the school was given the name Hilary Howse High School.

Hilary Howse was mayor of Nashville from 1909 until 1915. He served again as mayor from 1923 until 1938. Howse died in January of 1938. He died with only one memorial from the city he had served so long.

Just before his death, the new and fine high school out in West End was named Hilary Howse High School. Shortly after his death, however, students at the school successfully petitioned the Board of Education to change the name to West End High School.

Hilary Howse lived in East Nashville at 607 North Fourteenth Street. But, he also had a summer home in Haysboro which was a resort community back in those days in what is now North Inglewood and the National Cemetery section of Madison.

I was told that Hilary Howse had his desk in the front entrance of the courthouse and greeted everyone who came in. That was a little unusual for a mayor.

———— • ————

Did you know that the first electric streetcar made its first trip out West End Avenue to Vanderbilt University in 1889?

Do you remember the large Coca-Cola sign which sat up high where Broadway and West End Avenue forks at 16th Avenue? Also, at one time there was a horse water trough at that location.

Do you remember Wally Fowler? He was a nationally known promoter of gospel and country music who organized the first "All-night Sing" at the Ryman Auditorium on November 8, 1948.

Do you remember Roger Miller's King of the Road Motel downtown off of the Interstate? That was Ronnie Milsap's first performing job after moving from Memphis to Nashville.

I am sure you have seen Walt Disney's *Jungle Book*. I have seen it a million times with my grandchildren. They can sing every song, and so can I. The voice of Baloo the Bear in the movie was done by Tennessee-born Phil Harris.

If you have read any of Alfred Leland Crabb's historical novels about Nashville, then you have read about various turnpikes coming in and out of Old Nashville. In fact, you can read the historical marker out in front of the fire hall close to 21st Avenue and Blair Boulevard, and realize that spot as being the location of the toll house on the old Hillsboro Turnpike.

Tolls were collected on many of the early Tennessee roads at gates made of long poles called "pikes" that could be "turned" out of the way to allow a horse or coach to pass. So, it was only natural to call those roads "turnpikes."

Clyde Lee who by some has been called the top basketball player of all time at Vanderbilt. Clyde was a 6'9" center at Vandy from 1964 until 1966 who later became a player for the Philadelphia 76ers.

And, you remember Tracy Caulkins who won the gold medal in swimming at the 1984 Olympics.

Do you remember when our Union Station was busy with passengers coming and going and making train connections? Do you remember the Red Caps at the depot?

The N. C. & St. L. railroad put into service a real speedster named the City of Memphis to replace an older train called The Volunteer. It was built in the West Nashville shops off of Charlotte Avenue near Centennial Park. The train was really special. It had reclining seats, picture windows, and air-conditioning. Travel time was cut to about five hours between Nashville and Memphis.

I can remember when I was a child that I often went with my father, a railroader, to the old office building of the Nashville, Chattanooga and St. Louis Railroad which stood on the north side of Broadway near Tenth Avenue. My father had to go there often to have his railroad watch checked for accuracy. Back in those days, a railroader's watch was very important to the function of his duties.

That building was torn down. In that general area today is a hotel on one corner of Tenth Avenue and Broadway, and the Baptist Bookstore was built on another corner across the street. By the way, today, Baptist Bookstores are called LifeWay Christian stores.

Do you remember when the old Union Station train shed and part of the Union Station Hotel were damaged in a fire? That was in June of 1996. Of course, the whole shed has been torn down since then.

How many of you remember when the WSM television studios and tower were located on the hill above Compton and Bernard Avenues behind Belmont University? In 1957 the station had erected a new TV tower at 38th and Dakota Avenues in West Nashville. When the tower was nearing completion, it collapsed to the ground. There were four men killed during the accident.

In 1958, another transmitter and tower were constructed on Stephens' Hill on Knob Road just west of White Bridge Road. The tower is 1,368 feet tall, and it weighs 180 tons. In September of 1963, new WSM-TV studios were constructed on

Knob Road.

Did you watch the TV series on the AMC channel called *Remember WENN?* Anyone who loves old radio had to watch that. It was AMC's first original series saluting the Golden Age of Radio.

Loew's Theatre burned in the 1960s, and later moved into the Crescent Theatre on Church Street between Fourth and Fifth Avenues becoming Loew's Crescent.

———— • ————

Griffin Supply Company, before being located on Middleton Avenue behind the old Sears-Roebuck store on Eighth Avenue South, was located at the corner of Fifth Avenue and Broadway. The store was beside Tootsie's Orchid Lounge, and the Ryman Auditorium was across the back alley from the store.

My sister, Elva F. Griffin, and my brother-in-law, John Owen Griffin, owned Griffin Supply Company. When Burt Reynolds did his movie titled *W. W. and the Dixie Dance Kings*, many scenes were shot out back of their store where musicians would enter the stage door to the Ryman. Also, they wanted scenes with musicians entering Tootsie's Orchid Lounge.

There was such a narrow space to set up the cameras and equipment back behind Tootsie's, they put a Tootsie's sign on the back door of Griffin Supply Company, and when musicians supposedly entered Tootsie's in the movie, they were really entering the back door of Griffin Supply Company.

Can you remember back when we used the term "country and western music?" Back in 1941, I was playing on a show at WLAC radio called *Ranch House Melodies.* Even Pee Wee King's group was known as The Golden West Cowboys.

Some of the western music was "I'm Back in the Saddle Again" by Gene Autry, "Bury Me Not on the Lone Prairie" by Tex Ritter, Marty Robbins did "The Streets of Laredo," "Happy Trails" was sung by Roy Rogers and Dale Evans, and the Sons of the Pioneers had big hits with "Cool Water," and "Tumbling Tumble Weed."

———— • ————

One of the most astonishing things we can see around Nashville is the high, double-arch bridge on the Natchez Trace Parkway over state highway 96 just southwest of Nashville.

It is the only bridge of its kind in the United States (and one of only two in the world.) My wife, sister, and I crossed over the post-tensioned, segmental concrete double-arch bridge when we drove the Natchez Trace Parkway with our church group from the Parkway's starting point in Nashville off of Highway 100 to Jackson, Mississippi, and then on to Vicksburg. Some of the road was still under construction.

While on the Parkway, you will drive near Hohenwald, Tennessee and the burial site of Meriwether Lewis. I am sure you recall many of the Lewis and Clark expeditions. Lewis County in Tennessee is named for him.

Back in the old days, Lewis was going from St. Louis to Washington along the old Natchez Trace. At sunset on October 11, 1810, Lewis reached an Inn at Grinder's Stand where he lodged for the night. How he died that night is still a mystery.

Captain Lewis is buried where he died, and the site is a National Landmark in the Meriwether Lewis Park at mile marker 385.9 on the Natchez Trace. The grave monument is in the shape of a broken column, a symbol of a life ended before it was fully lived.

———•———

Here are a few tid-bits that happened over the years which I believe will spark your nostalgic memories. In 1924, General Shoe Corporation was organized and became one of the world's largest companies of its kind. That same year, Scarritt College moved to Nashville from Kansas City, Missouri.

In 1933, many of us remember the East Nashville tornado. My uncle and aunt lived in East Nashville. My uncle's car was left sitting where it should have been in the garage, but the whole garage was gone. He has "never seen the garage since," as he would say.

In 1936, radio station WSIX moved to Nashville from Springfield, Tennessee. I was twelve years old, and I remember that I was at a neighbor's house playing board games with my friends. The father of the household had the correct frequency set on his AM radio dial, and we kept waiting for the station to come on the air. Sure enough, it was around seven o'clock that evening that we heard the first words over WSIX-AM radio broadcasting from Nashville.

In 1943, you may have gone to the movies and have seen *For Whom the Bell Tolls*, or *The Song of Bernadette*. I was in the Army, and I remember seeing *Stage Door Canteen*.

In 1954 *The Wonderful World of Disney* made its television debut on our television screens. In 1954, November 11th, which had been called "Armistice Day" since World War I, was renamed "Veterans Day" to honor veterans of all wars.

In 1956, the Old Hickory Lake was completed. And, in 1957, Tom Little, a cartoonist for *The Tennessean* newspaper received the Pulitzer prize. Also, this was the year that the 31-

story Life & Casualty building was completed at the corner of Fourth Avenue, North and Church Street.

During the decade of the 1950s, we read about the Brinks robbery. We went to drive-in movies. First-class postage was 4 cents to mail a letter. We had the happy experience of reading Red O'Donnell's entertaining column called "Top o' the Morning." Red's real name was Francis X. O'Donnell. Elvis had teen-age girls going ga-ga. Alaska and Hawaii were added as our 49th and 50th states. And, Dr. Seuss' *Cat in the Hat* delighted us all.

In 1962, the Municipal Auditorium was built. In 1963, the Metropolitan Government of Nashville-Davidson County was officially established. Beverly Briley became the first mayor of Metro Nashville. George H. Cate, Jr. became our first vice-mayor.

Broadway produced *Fiddler on the Roof.* We saw the movie *Dr. Zhivago.* Johnny Carson came to the *Tonight Show.*

All in the Family set a new type of ethnic and bathroom humor. And, do you remember the pet rocks and the mood rings?

In 1987, the gas-powered Nashville Trolleys came on the scene serving downtown, Music Row, and Music Valley. And, still, "Time Marches On."

If you enjoy TRIVIA, then here are a few tid-bits you can spring on someone: The old Maxwell House Hotel was named for Harriet Maxwell Overton, who was the wife of its builder, John Overton, Jr.

Did you ever know the price on the tag of Minnie Pearl's

hat she wore when performing on the *Grand Ole Opry*? It was $1.98. I have seen it.

Country music's Faron Young has the distinction of having his records heard all the way to the moon when Pete Conrad carried his tapes with him on the Apollo 12 mission.

Do you remember the *Camel Caravan* which entertained our troops during World War II? There was a *Grand Ole Opry Camel Caravan* also which traveled and performed for our service personnel around the world during World War II.

I am sure you have purchased some film or other photo supplies from Dury's. George Dury was a very famous Tennessee artist who painted a portrait of Mrs. James K. Polk that hangs today in the East Room of the White House.

The famous writer of short stories known as O. Henry was a guest at the old Maxwell House Hotel while paying a visit to his daughter, who was a student at Ward-Belmont finishing school for girls in Nashville.

When O. Henry (William Sydney Porter) departed from Nashville by train, he began writing a story about Nashville as he was crossing the Cumberland River on the old railroad trestle. The name of the story is *A Municipal Report*.

Do you know what made the clock in the Union Station tower unique at the time of its construction? The clock was digital, and the numerals were mounted on movable cloth strips.

Edward E. Barnard was a native Nashvillian who was a celestial photographer and astronomer. He is noted for discovering the fifth moon of Jupiter in 1892.

The Tennessee School for the Blind was created in 1843

by a man named James Chaplin. Back then it was just a small school. Later, the facility became a state school funded by the Tennessee Department of Education.

In 1853, a new school building was constructed on Lebanon Pike in an area which we now call Donelson. However, during the Civil War, the building was used as a military hospital and it was almost destroyed.

Nashvillian John M. Lea bought the old Claiborne mansion on Fillmore Street which is now called Hermitage Avenue. Lea donated the property to the state for the school, and the Tennessee School for the Blind stayed there for almost 80 years.

In 1952, the fine school was moved to its present location at 115 Stewarts Ferry Pike.

———————◆———————

Our great, old Paramount Theatre featured the giant, three-manual organ rising on hydraulic lifts up to stage level between shows, and to accompany the audience in singing to the bouncing ball on the screen.

The Paramount Theatre was built in 1930 with its $50,000 three-manual Wurlitzer console installed. I understand that the first organist to play the organ was a man who went by the showmanship name of "C. Sharp Minor." He was hired to play for the first four weeks of the theatre's showings in 1930. He was followed by a man named Jack Thurston.

Also, very early the organ was played by Mary Elizabeth Hicks with whom I worked at WLAC radio. I was talking to my good friend of many years, Otto Bash, who was a musician all of his life like I, and Otto told me that he had seen a photo of Mary Liz playing the organ at the Paramount Theatre in 1930.

Another organist to play at the Paramount was Leon Cole, and one of the last organists to play at the theatre was Bob Luck.

The theatre was sold in 1978 to the Martin Theatre chain. And, the great, old theatre was torn down in the 1980s. Many of us still hold fond memories of that great old show place.

National Stores and Paramount Theatre on Church Street (1957)

We lived in Evansville, Indiana in the mid-1960s while I was on the music department faculty of Evansville College. One evening, one of our friends said, "Get in my car. I want to take you somewhere and show you something."

This friend took us to a home of one of his friends who we learned was a repairer and collector of organs. This gentleman took us down into a large basement where we saw many organs in a varied state of repair. The man sat down at one of the organ keyboards and began to play.

I was pleasantly shocked and surprised when the man said, "This is an organ that was in the Paramount Theatre in Nashville, Tennessee!"

Today, I don't know the person's address in Evansville or even remember his name. I have always wondered if that organ collector was mistaken, or if that organ really had been in the Paramount Theatre. It sounded like the organ in the Paramount Theatre. It may have been there in his basement for repair at the time. Maybe I really did get to see the keyboard and hear that old organ from my childhood.

———— • ————

Advertising today is something totally different from our old days. Today, I can look at a commercial on the television screen, and I have no idea what company or product it is advertising. Then, at the end of the 30-second spot, they flash the name of the product on the screen for what seems to be less than a second.

In the old days, we knew what the product being advertised was from the start. We even associated a product with a one-liner that we could always remember. For instance, all of you remember hearing "A little dab will do ya." We knew that was Brylcream. When Pepsodent toothpaste was advertised, we knew that we would hear "You'll wonder where the yellow went."

All of us knew that "Better things for better living through chemistry" was referring to DuPont. "Fire-Chief gasoline" was Texaco. I remember when we had the Saturday night boxing on television sponsored by Gillette Blue Blades, and we heard the announcer say "Look sharp, feel sharp, be sharp."

We knew that Colgate toothpaste "Cleans your breath while it cleans your teeth." Dinah Shore used to sing "See the USA in your Chevrolet." "Quick, Henry, the Flit" was familiar. My wife and I just ate some Campbell's Soup, and my wife said, "Mmm, Mmm, good!" And, if you don't know "Good to the last drop," then you have never read my column in the *Westview* Newspaper!

———— •◆• ————

In old East Nashville, John Shelby was a physician and businessman. Also, he was the founder of Shelby Medical School in Nashville. Dr. John Shelby once owned the land that is now Shelby Park.

Around the turn of the 20th century, a real estate company purchased the land which the company considered prime for residential development. To create interest in that section, it was decided to build an amusement park named for the early 19th century physician Dr. John Shelby. The park had a roller coaster, offered band concerts, dances and picnics, boat rides, balloon ascensions, and horseback riding.

Unfortunately, the development firm went bankrupt in 1903. The Nashville Park Commission took an immediate interest in the site. Shelby Park opened as a public facility for citizens in 1912.

Major Eugene C. Lewis was a brilliant civic leader, and at that period of time was a prime force on the Park Commission. He was a civil engineer in charge of planning for Nashville, Chattanooga and St. Louis Railroad routes. Also, Major Lewis was a big influence and inspiration for the Tennessee 100th Anniversary Exposition held in West Side Park (which is today called Centennial Park). Lewis later drafted the development plan for Shelby Park.

It was Major E. C. Lewis' ideas to include a real Dutch windmill, a concrete boat-house on Lake Sevier that resembled the front of a steamboat, and Sycamore Lodge sitting down near the Cumberland River. I remember well all three of those structures, but none of them exist today. Old Windmill Hill sits now in the park covered with grass, brush, and trees. The old Dutch windmill was said to have burned; however, its real demise was never fully explained. Sycamore Lodge was demolished in 1984. And, the concrete boat-house on Lake Sevier was torn down. The Park Commission has improved the lake surroundings and has added spraying fountains to help beautify the area.

Today in our present Nashville, we have many fine innovators of ideas for the structural development of our city. One hundred years from now, it would be interesting to see how they are written up in history books, and the credit they are given for the development of Nashville during the 21st century.

A true Southerner knows that "fixin'" can be used as a noun, a verb, or an adverb. And, only a true Southerner knows exactly how long "directly" is—as in the sentence: "I'm going to town, be back directly."

And, while I am on the subject, did you know that only a true Southerner can show or point out to you the general direction of "yonder."

And, please, true Southerners never, never refer to one person as Y'all. And, by the way, a true Southerner knows you don't scream obscenities at little old ladies who drive 20 MPH on the Interstate. You just say, "Bless her heart," and go on your way.

Do you remember when we took autograph books to school so our friends could sign them with a silly saying or rhyme? And, silly they were!

"When Cupid shoots his arrow, I hope he Mrs. you."

"Can't think, brain dumb, inspiration won't come, bad ink, bad pen, best wishes, Amen."

"When you get married and have twins, don't come to me for safety pins."

"My little heart is like a cabbage, easily broken in two. The leaves I'll give to anyone, but the heart I'll give to you."

Most of the sayings were silly and made little sense, but it was fun.

"When you get older and move to town, if a boy tries to kiss you, just politely knock him down."

"Tell your Mom to hold her tongue; she had a beau when she was young. Tell your Dad to do the same; he was the one who changed her name."

Also, there were a few people who liked to be serious when signing your autograph book or writing in your school annual:

"Deem it not an idle thing, a pleasant word to speak; the face you wear, the thought you bring, a heart may heal or break."

"Your eyes are like diamonds, your teeth are like pearls, your lips are like rubies, you're a jewel of a girl."

Allow me one more in my reminiscing: "When the golden sun is setting, and your heart from care is free, when o'er a thousand things you're thinking, will you sometimes think of me?" And, please don't anyone yell BURMA SHAVE!

———•———

I hope this smorgasbord of **Times, People, Places and Things** brings some nice nostalgic tastes and memories back to you with a relish of happiness.

Stay healthy and happy, everybody!

We could sit and cry about "the good old days," but instead, we need to look to the future for even greater things to come.

A marvelous, shining future is awaiting us!

Index of Names

272

Index of Businesses, Institutions, Places and Things

Photo Credits

pp. 36, 47, 114, 209, and book cover – Courtesy of Tennessee State Library and Archives

pp. 23, 39, 187, 188, 210, 212, 221, and 260 – Courtesy of Metropolitan Government Archives of Nashville and Davidson County

pp. 13 and 143 – Courtesy of Nashville Association of Musicians, AFM Local 257

pp. 134 and 135 – Courtesy of Jeff Thompson

p. 94 – Courtesy of Otto Bash

p. vi – Photo by Jeff Thompson

pp. 120 and 245 – Photos by Sonia Young Thompson

pp. 32, 33, 118, 119, and 179 – Photos by E. D. Thompson

pp. 57, 66, 76 and 80 – Unknown

Also available by E.D. Thompson

$19.95

ISBN 0-9744322-3-7

Available online at www.westviewpublishing.com

Ordering Additional Copies

To order additional copies of More Nashville Nostalgia or Nashville Nostalgia, please complete the form below and mail with your payment to:

Westview Publishing Co., Inc.
P.O. Box 210183
Nashville, TN 37221

Your mailing address:

Name: ⎯⎯⎯⎯⎯⎯⎯⎯⎯⎯⎯⎯⎯⎯⎯

Address: ⎯⎯⎯⎯⎯⎯⎯⎯⎯⎯⎯⎯⎯

City: ⎯⎯⎯⎯⎯⎯⎯⎯⎯⎯⎯⎯⎯⎯⎯

State: ⎯⎯⎯⎯⎯⎯⎯⎯ Zipcode: ⎯⎯⎯⎯⎯

Telephone: ⎯⎯⎯⎯⎯⎯⎯⎯⎯⎯⎯⎯

Amount you need to enclose:

Nashville Nostalgia:⎯⎯ copies at $19.95 ⎯⎯⎯⎯

More Nashville Nostalgia: ⎯⎯ copies at $19.95 ⎯⎯⎯⎯

Tax at 9.25% (TN residents only) ⎯⎯⎯⎯

$4.00 S&H for the 1st book ⎯⎯⎯⎯

$2.00 S&H for ea. additional book ⎯⎯⎯⎯

Total amount enclosed: ⎯⎯⎯⎯

**Also available to purchase online at
www.westviewpublishing.com**

Printed in the United States
38838LVS00002B/175-225

9 780975 564677